MELATI WIJSEN

CHANGE STARTS NOW

100 LESSONS FROM A FULL-TIME CHANGEMAKER

Cover image by: Stuart Sullivan
Author photo: © Carmen Kemmink
Typesetting: Mat-Zet B.V.

Printed in the United Kingdom
First Printing, 2025

ISBN: 978-981-94-2668-3 (Paperback)
ISBN: 978-981-94-2669-0 (Colour Hardback)

YOUTHTOPIA PTE LTD
Singapore 068914

youthtopiapublishing@gmail.com

This is for all 12-year-olds out there
who dare to do something different.
And for those a bit older and younger,
who are curious too.

A few questions to make us wonder:

Do you remember being 12 years old?
What were you like?
What were you curious about?
What made your heart beat so fast
it shook the ground beneath your feet?

THE FLOW OF THE BOOK

ABOUT THIS CHANGEMAKER

Full name: Melati Riyanto Wijsen

Date of birth: 19th December, 2000

Job: Full-time changemaker

My definition of a changemaker: A changemaker is anybody who wakes up in the morning and thinks, "What can I do today to make the world around me better?"

Projects worked on: Bye Bye Plastic Bags, Mountain Mamas, One Island One Voice, Bali's Biggest Clean Up, *Bigger Than Us* the movie, and YOUTHTOPIA

Nationality: I'm a mixed kid! My parents are Indonesian & Dutch

Home: Between Bali and Amsterdam

Biggest live audience: 9,000 people, Ziggo Dome, Amsterdam, 2023

Passion(s): Telling stories, listening to music, and going to thrift stores and markets

Diet: Vegetarian – yes, for environmental reasons

Star sign: Sagittarius

Fears: Heights, the dark, and disappointing people

Family: Isabel a.k.a. Bel (younger sister), Elvira (mama), Eko (papa)

The thing I'm most proud of: Being brave enough at 12 years old to take action. I have no clue where I would be, or who I would be, if it weren't for the courage of my 12-year-old self. I thank her every day.

Saturday, 13-10-2012
I was 11 years old, moments before my life changed,
when I wrote this.

A Poem: Last Seed on Earth

If I had the last seed in my hands,
I would call a band
to play a song
while I run into the center of town
not to receive a crown
but to plant this seed in the ground,
from the tip of my forehead
I can feel the heavy drops of excitement
dripping
panting, panting, panting
I made it
pulling out my kit
I shove the shovel into the warm
silky soil
that has been waiting for this moment to happen,
gently placing the seed in its comfy new home
when suddenly everything looked
much much
more
green

FOREWORD

When a twelve-year-old girl from Bali decided she could no longer accept seeing her beautiful island drowning in plastic, she didn't wait for permission to act. She didn't wait for the "right time" or for someone else to solve the problem. Melati Wijsen simply began. This is exactly the kind of defiant optimism our world desperately needs right now.

I have spent decades working on climate action, including leading the Paris Agreement negotiations, and I can tell you with absolute certainty: the most powerful force for change today is not coming from conference rooms or corridors of power. It's coming from young leaders like Melati who combine vision with unstoppable determination.

What makes this book so vital is not so much that it is a story about youth activism, but rather that it is a practical blueprint for turning passion into impact.

Through 100 honest, hard-won lessons, Melati shows us that changemaking isn't about waiting for perfect conditions or having all the answers. It's about starting where you are, with what you have, right now.

When I look at Melati's journey – from organizing island-wide cleanups to speaking on global stages – I see the kind of leadership our climate emergency demands. This is not leadership that asks permission or waits for validation. This is leadership that springs from a deep understanding that when we see something wrong in our world, we have not just the right, but the responsibility to act.

To the young person reading this book: you might feel overwhelmed by the scale of challenges we face. You might wonder if your actions can really make a difference in a world where we need to transform entire systems. I understand that, but I have learned that great transformation begins with someone refusing to accept the world as it is.

The beauty of Melati's approach – and what makes this book so powerful – is that she breaks down the journey of changemaking into actionable steps that anyone can follow.

Whether you're concerned about plastic pollution, climate change, social justice, or any other issue that keeps you up at night, these lessons provide a road map for turning that concern into meaningful action.

We are living in the decisive decade for humanity. The actions we take – or fail to take – in the coming years will determine the world that future generations will inherit. That's why we need more young leaders who understand that change starts with a decision: the decision to begin, to persist, to rise above setbacks, and to inspire others to join the journey.

This book is more than a guide – it's an invitation to join a growing global family of change leaders who believe in their power to shape the future. As you read Melati's story and absorb her lessons, you will realize that no one is too young, too inexperienced, or too anything to make a difference. The world cannot afford to wait for someone else to solve its problems. The time for action is now, and you – yes, you – are exactly who we've been waiting for.

Change starts now. Are you ready to begin?

Christiana Figueres,

Executive Secretary UN Climate Change Convention 2010-2016

INTRODUCTION

Some will call this book a coming-of-age story, some would call it a reflection of growth, and others will call it an inspiring life story. Well, this is my story, which, if I'm being honest, has become one of hundreds of thousands of young people's stories today. But I have what they call a track record. I've been a changemaker for more than half of my life. It is all I know to be.

It started when a brave 12-year-old girl from Bali had a vision to make her island home plastic bag free.

You see, when I started my first organization, Bye Bye Plastic Bags, there was this:

- Beauty of not caring what others thought
- Clarity of knowing what I wanted
- Absurd simplicity of doing the right thing for the right reason

It was as simple as that. Now, as I sit here, writing away, I'm not sure I have it in me anymore. I want everything to be perfect all the time. I don't know where that brave, little 12-year-old girl went. I sometimes forget that I used to be her.

So, I'll tell you what this book is. It's a project for me to find the 12-year-old Melati again. Through sharing my story with you, I hope that somewhere along the way, maybe we both can find what once used to be and reconnect with the courage we know we still have and desperately need to create a world we believe in.

Each chapter consists of a few different elements. It's advised to read them in order, but some chapters are okay as standalone guides. Each chapter comes complete with:

- Real-life stories
- The lessons learned
- Questions to think about

I purposefully created the book in this way because I wanted to craft a learning journey for you while reading, but also create a space for you to reflect and take these lessons into your own every-day actions.

Whether you are someone like me, a young changemaker, or you are a business leader, high school teacher, or just someone interested in making change, this book is for you. It's a story of change, how to navigate it, make sense of it, and accelerate it.

As I began to write the book, one lesson came up after another. Today, what you are holding in your hands is a book with 100 lessons in total. It's a lot, it's chaotic, sometimes confrontational, but that is what the journey of a young changemaker is all about. And besides, the biggest lesson of all is that our lives are a constant learning journey. Even as I write the end of the introduction, I can think of 10 more lessons I could've added. But see this as a start: 100 lessons now, and at the end, start creating your own list. Implement what you learn. Put it into practice and share it loudly with others. We must learn from each other to accelerate change. Add your story to #ChangeStartsNow and be a part of a global community of like-minded people.

We do not have the luxury of time to waste. Change *must* start now.

Changemaking and young people taking action have become dinner table conversations in so many households today. Our generation is making waves, finding ways to be part of a better world. This book belongs in that category.

But I want to show you what it's like – what it takes. The building of that wave until the crash on the sand. The sunrise and sunset of every memorable and not so memorable day in the life of a changemaker – and even better, how to become one.

I also wanted to say thank you for being here, and thank you for picking up this book. This *book*!! Oh my, I still can't believe it's a real life, actual book! So yes, from deep in my heart, a massive thank you from me to you.

Most importantly, though, I want this story to be yours. I want you to read it and see yourself in these pages. Because not only is it possible, but it already is true. The fact that you have this book shows that you are hungry and ready for the truth, insights, the how, the why. All of it. And I will do my very best to tell you the truth as it has been for me, from when I started at 12 years old to this day.

This book holds 100 lessons from over a decade at the front lines of change. It's been one crazy adventure, and I can't wait to share it with you.

So let's get started.

With so much love,
Melati Riyanto Wijsen

CHAPTER ONE:

THE CURIOUS 12-YEAR-OLD

Lessons in this chapter:

#1: We are nature

#2: We protect what we love

#3: Balance between good and bad creates harmony

#4: Tri Hita Karana

#5: Feeling safe allows you to explore

#6: Always ask questions

#7: Role Models Matter

#8: Find your focus

#9: Change takes time

The early morning sun was soft and gently fell into our open living room which faced directly into our garden. Birds were waking up, and you could hear them start their songs. There was a gentle breeze from the ocean starting to pick up. There was a calmness at home, surrounded by green rice fields and a clear view of the Balinese heart, Mount Agung.

This was my favorite time of the day. Our family home has a high ceiling held up by long, white pillars. My mother always tells the story of when they built the house. She could barely speak the local language. So, in their meetings, she would use body language to say how she wanted a high ceiling to allow the natural light to fall in. She stood there, she said, motioning "up, up, up," hoping they understood her crazy moves upwards. Luckily, they did. I always wish I could've seen that moment. It resulted in the house I love so much. To ensure the openness and natural light of our home, the entire front of the house is open. We never had a front door. It was as if our home had open, outstretched arms, inviting the rice fields into our living room. It fit the philosophy that our parents raised us with: we were one with nature.

Ancient, mismatched furniture filled each corner. Mama's buddha shrine in one corner, Papa's symbolic Islam star in the other. There was a TV that we never turned on. It was in front of the wooden bed that my parents cut in half to turn into our couch. The center of the house was our wooden dinner table, complete with its mismatched chairs around it. Every night, we would sit there for hours, exchanging stories and contemplating questions.

On the right side of the house, we have a veranda peering over our garden and directly next to it, the village temple stands next to an ancient banyan tree. I sat crisscrossed in the morning crisp air, mesmerized by the magic of this big, living, breathing tree. It was so peaceful. It was so beautiful. It was so grounding. I remember thinking, "I want to be like you when I grow up, tree."

I found a comfortable spot to sit on the veranda, admiring the tree in this golden morning light. I heard my sister come out of our room, and she joined me where I sat on the veranda. We both smiled widely as we looked at each other.

Our shirts were matching. Last night, the shirts for our campaign had arrived. We were so excited for the sun to come up to see them in this light. They looked better than we could have ever imagined.

"Ready?" I asked my 10-year-old sister.

She nodded, and we helped each other up as we heard our mum in the kitchen preparing breakfast.

"Girls, breakfast is ready! We have to be in the car in 20 minutes, otherwise you'll be late for school."

"Coming!"

We walked over proudly in our campaign shirts to show our parents just how good they looked.

"Look at you two!" our parents beamed.

After we finished breakfast, we grabbed our school bags, our homework from last night, and the lunch boxes that were waiting on the kitchen table and headed to the car.

"Wait!" I said. "Can you take a picture?"

I wanted to remember this moment forever.

My sister and I dropped our bags, ran to the temple in front of our magical tree, and proudly stood side by side. We puffed our chests out, so anyone who ever looked back at this moment could see our mission clearly. Our shirts read: *Bye Bye Plastic Bags.*

This was day one of our mission, which entirely embodied our purpose. This was where it began. Right there. I felt so proud. I felt it bursting out of me. At 10 and 12 years old, we were ready to do the right thing.

There was no turning back now.

LESSON #1: WE ARE NATURE

To me, my parents are like superheroes. At first glance, my mother and I look nothing alike. She's blonde, I'm brunette; her blue eyes, my brown eyes. And yet, the longer you look, the stronger the similarities appear. And the longer you get to know us, you start to wonder if the saying "the apple doesn't fall far from the tree" was made to describe us.

My father was raised in Surabaya, the second largest city on the island of Java, and he is the eldest of seven siblings. So, he carries the weight and the responsibility of being the eldest sibling. At the same time, he was the best at playing games with us all day long as kids.

Our parents raised us so we were constantly surrounded by nature: at home we were around rice fields and had a big tree in our living room, at school we were in the middle of the jungle, or on holidays we would go on the ocean on my favorite boat.

The Ombak Putih is a traditional boat, complete with big, beautiful sails and a wide wooden deck. It was painted white and dark blue, to match its name: Ombak putih translates to "white wave" in Indonesian. My parents met while working on the boat at the same time. My dad was the purser and took care of guest relations. My mother had a similar role, but she was more on the operations and planning side of things.

During my childhood, our family spent a lot of time sailing through the 17,000 islands of my home country. It wasn't all-year-long, although it sometimes felt like it as a kid. We would spend a couple of weeks at a time on the boat throughout the year. My sister's first steps were taken on a beach of a remote island. And one of my favorite things was falling asleep with the sound of waves softly lapping the sides of the boat. These sounds became the soundtrack and lullaby I think back to whenever I have trouble sleeping. Each day felt like a new adventure because every morning we would wake up in a different part of the country, meaning my sister and I would have new "worlds" to explore. We would race each other out of the cabins and climb up onto the deck, peering out to see what we could identify: trees, hills, people, and dolphins.

The ocean carried us through our childhood. Looking back, the time spent onboard the boat feels magical. Jumping off the deck and playing games from sunrise to sunset, our imagination was at its peak. We formed a deep love and understanding for the big blue. These adventures built the foundation for the explorer mindset my sister and I now have, as well as deepened our understanding of how interconnected we are to nature. We are not separate from it.

Every day, we would end our days at the beach watching the sun go down, and our parents would share the craziest stories and myths. They would let us imagine how lakes came to be (the fairytale of Danau Toba), or why stealing from gardens is never a good idea (Kancil and the Timun). But most of all, they would mix in lessons that I still think about every day.

"Girls, take a deep breath," we'd hear one day as the setting sun turned the sky pink and orange.

As my sister and I both took a few deep breaths in and out, my father asked: "Did you know that the ocean gives us oxygen?"

"Don't trees in the rainforests give us oxygen?" we questioned, because that's what we were taught in school. Trees and plants go through a cycle of photosynthesis, capture our CO_2, and in return provide oxygen.

"That is true," my mum jumped in, "but 70% of oxygen comes from the ocean." She went on to explain that these tiny little creatures on the surface of the ocean called phytoplankton produce oxygen for us to breathe. They are the leaves and trees of the ocean.

"70%? That's so much!"

"Yes girls, it means that every other breath you take comes from the ocean. Always remember that. We must treat our oceans with care and respect."

We never looked at the ocean the same again. From that point on, we felt connected to this large being of water that literally keeps us alive. We are nature.

EXPLORING. DISCOVERING. QUESTIONING.

I know a big reason for why I do what I do today is because of those very moments when my parents raised my awareness of how lucky, how beautiful, and how special each and every breath of life is. I learned to protect what I love.

LESSON #2: WE PROTECT WHAT WE LOVE

The foundation of our love for nature was starting to build. It was strong. We loved the ocean, we loved the wind blowing through our hair while we sailed around the country. We loved the rain, the trees, and the pristine beaches. Sure, we were island kids running around the rice fields and climbing trees most days, but I could already feel a strong sense of self and connection to the natural beauty around me. When I would see a tree being cut down, I would cry. When I got the chance to learn and build a garden bed at school, I wished it was my real bed to sleep in.

Naturally, we protect what we love. We don't want to see it hurt, or sad, or destroyed. When we are clear about what we love, we know we will do everything in our power to protect it. It is so fundamental to create experiences and spaces where we allow ourselves to fall in love with nature.

LOVE. PROTECT. NURTURE.

Essentially, there are two reasons why I am this way. My parents and Bali. If I had grown up anywhere else in the world, I'm not sure I would have had the chance to explore with so much creativity, become the person I wanted to be, and envision the world I wanted to create.

LESSON #3: BALANCE BETWEEN GOOD AND BAD CREATES HARMONY

Next to the magic of its nature, Bali is known for its magical ceremonies. The culture in which we grew up was unique. Bali is believed to be an island floating on the back of a turtle. There are magical spirits and elements roaming around the lands and seas.

"Selalu ingat ya Melati."

"Always remember Melati," a local villager would tell me one day, unknowingly about to teach me my next lesson. "In Bali, we believe that everything must be given gratitude. The world of good and bad is one." He looked up at the sky as he paused, while I eagerly waited for him to continue.

"We must always remain in balance. We must never get too greedy. We must always worship the good and the bad together, otherwise the island will fall out of its balance."

Balance quickly became an anchor in the way I tried to look at things. Ever heard that saying: energy flows where the attention goes? Too much of anything is never good. So the Balinese believe in worshipping the good and the bad to create a reality of balance.

In Bali, there are a series of important, recurring ceremonies like Galungan, Kuningan, and Melasti. There is a ceremony for everything. One for cleansing, one for animals, one for asking permission to start building on land or to move into a new house, and there's even one for car and motorbike safety on the road.

There are ceremonies that last a whole day, with weeks of preparation leading up to these prayers. The villages all over the island decorate their homes with a penjor, a wooden arch decorated with dried leaves and flowers that are woven in patterns to show a sign of celebration. The Balinese dress in beautiful, traditional outfits, in yellow and white or black and white squares. In the temples, high priests lead prayers, and holy water is passed around for members to cleanse themselves of all the bad emotions, and create space for the old and new. Each ceremony brings balance back into practice.

Next to the nature and the ceremonies, growing up in Bali also built a deep awareness within. At a young age, an awareness settled of knowing that you are part of something bigger. We are never alone. We learned how to create space to learn and to listen to others. We watched elements of nature be celebrated as if they were our gods, our teachers. We honored the lessons of the sea and the evilness of greed and disruption of balance.

BALANCE. AWARENESS. HARMONY.

Bali made me who I am today. When I first started my activism, I rooted myself a lot in the energy of Bali. Without knowing, I was slowly introduced to the basic concept of sustainability: how we can live in balance with the natural world around us. We must not only take, take, take, but we must also give: the true harmony and relationship between people and planet.

LESSON #4: TRI HITA KARANA

Tri Hita Karana is a way of life that embodies exactly that. Tri Hita Karana is what living in balance and harmony truly looks like.

"Melati jangan lupa," a village member told me. "Melati, do not forget."

"Long ago, we followed a lifestyle on our island. One we have lost touch with, but one that should always be remembered. Do you know what it is, Melati?"

As I was only a child and unsure of how to answer, I stayed quiet.

They continued, "*Tri Hita Karana.* It is how we should live every day. It is the way of life where we live in balance and harmony with three very important elements. Balance between us and the environment, us amongst each other, and last but not least, balance with the spirit within."

Tri Hita Karana.

Slowly, I started to nod. This made *sense.* I felt like I had heard this before. This was so obviously what the world needed. I felt I had already known of Tri Hita Karana somewhere deep down in my bones.

"I will never forget," I said.

Tri Hita Karana.

How can each of us implement this formula for a balanced, respectful, kind, sustainable lifestyle? It is something that has existed for generations and something that desperately needs to be practiced again.

I was obsessed with the concept. I kept trying to understand how we could have had this way of life and suddenly lost touch. If it once was, how do we get back to that moment?

It already exists! The answer is Tri Hita Karana. I loved listening to our village elders and the stories of the Balinese and Indonesian culture. I made a decision to implement Tri Hita Karana in as many aspects of my life as I could.

Had I contributed enough to the community today?

How was my interaction with nature today?

Did I create enough space for myself today?

In this way, breaking it down to these three simple areas of life, following the principles of Tri Hita Karana, helped me navigate and create a lifestyle for myself that was sustainable and balanced.

Self-awareness and a "Bigger Than Us" mindset were already built into my DNA, but we are not taught enough about it until too late in life. This is a shame, because it's also such a hard thing to navigate, too. A lot of what makes me who I am today is the early awareness I had of how my actions, thoughts, or emotions can influence my own path. This awareness is power itself.

ENVIRONMENT. COMMUNITY. SELF.

LESSON #5: FEELING SAFE ALLOWS YOU TO EXPLORE

Whenever we were not sailing on the boat or having conversations with village elders, my sister and I were with our best friends in the village, Mya and Sasha.

They lived a few houses down the road, and our afternoons and mornings were filled with adventure. We'd go out exploring on our bicycles, packing our bags with water and snacks. Sometimes we would even bring pillows with us.

We seriously thought our little village was so big that we might have to camp out because we never knew when we would make it home. The funny thing is that when we got older, our parents told us that the villagers would always communicate back to them at every moment.

"They are at the warung buying snacks now."

"The girls just passed by the temple."

"They're back on the beach."

We had our own little protection bubble to grow up in. Community is everything, and without that safety, we wouldn't be where we are today because we couldn't have explored the way that we did.

Growing up with a feeling of safety and immense privilege, I also felt a great responsibility to pay attention. I was not raised to be ignorant. I was not taught to hide. I always asked difficult questions and went on adventures to find those answers, no matter what they might be. Fear did not stop me.

A shift happened at 12 years old. My home, that I loved so much and that had taught me so much, was under threat. The island was out of balance. Our Tri Hita Karana was gone. Our collective lifestyle began destroying the natural world instead of living in harmony with it. We were becoming greedy with short-term overconsumption. We no longer valued the long-term vision and balance of a healthy, sustainable, balanced ecosystem. Our definition of success and development started to mean and look like something else.

At school, I started to learn about many things that I wanted to pay more attention to.

A Diary Entry
29th September, 2012. I was 11 years old.

Dear Diary,

Today I was in charge of raising awareness at school about plastic, and I was so surprised by what I heard from some people. A boy said to me, "What are we collecting plastic for?" So I answered, "If you give plastic bags to an organization, we get money, and we give that money to charity."

"Oh for charity? Never mind, I'm going to be rich!"

I was so shocked and almost had to laugh because he was so selfish. I felt as if I was the only tree standing in the middle of a desert. But when I counted the plastic bags, it was more than 1000!

I'm sure the ground will crack and more trees will sprout; they just need a lot of water from me.

CURIOSITY. SAFETY. ACTION.

This experience at such a young age set me off to explore why people thought this way and what we could do to empower them to take action. I knew this work would need all of us.

Bali was choking under plastic pollution. It had come to a point where we, Indonesia as a country, had become the second largest source of marine plastic pollution. Right after China, Indonesia was runner up for contributing the most waste that destroys our oceans.

"Remember girls, we have to care for and respect our oceans, because every second breath comes from the ocean."

Every breath suddenly felt like it was suffocating me. The more I learned about how bad the problem was, the harder it became to breathe. I kept thinking about what we learned about growing up, our connection to nature and the importance of nature, the balance between good and bad, Tri Hita Karana. Nature fills our lungs with the air we need to stay alive. It feeds us, makes us happy, and cares for us. We have to protect it with everything we have. Clearly, we were not doing this. The oceans and the land were not receiving this care or respect from us at all.

The first time I really saw our destruction on a mass scale was when I visited Bali's largest landfill at the time: Suwung. I was 12 years old, and I saw hundreds of families living in or around the landfill. I remember throwing up all over my shoes, and it wasn't from the smell or the heat. Flies were everywhere, eating away at the rotting material. Old food, liquids, the most disgusting things you could imagine were a reality right there.

In that moment, a flood of questions came, one after the other. The beginning of my next lesson: curiosity shapes who we become. We must always follow the path of our questioning to know who we are and what we may one day become.

LESSON #6: ALWAYS ASK QUESTIONS

As I walked deeper into the center of the landfill, one question kept on repeating inside my head:

Why did we cause this much destruction?

I could hear the crunch of plastic beneath my shoes. The sun was glaring down, unforgiving. I couldn't believe what I was looking at. I didn't want to accept what I was seeing. Cows grazed on the ground, trying to find food in between the plastic. Birds circled above, and in the wind there were many plastic bags flying. I covered my nose, and my eyes filled with tears.

It was the first time I had experienced a broken heart.

How could we let this happen?

I didn't know what to do with myself. I was shaking and suddenly I lost all sense of direction. The only thing I could see was plastic. Mountains of trash taller than any building I had ever seen in my short life on the island. There was so much of it. All of this in a place out of sight, that nobody knows much about it. At 12 years old, I stood there thinking:

What can we do?

I suddenly realized my friend was standing a few meters behind me, and I remembered why we were here. Our goal had been to document and tell this story to the world. We were on an assignment that we had given ourselves: to learn more about the plastic problem. Now, our job was to capture the truth of where the island's trash ended up. Nobody could have prepared us for this.

Why did we not know about this sooner?

It didn't matter that I didn't know about this sooner. All that mattered was that I now knew. This was supposed to be a problem that was "out of sight, out of mind." But now that I knew, it was my mission to make every single person know, too. We were going to put it in the spotlight. It could never leave anyone's mind. I remember turning to the camera and speaking about the world we have created, where the "throw away" culture has become normal. But the question really is, where is "away"?

Out of sight, out of mind. We get away with so much as long as we are not confronted by it. Ignorance is comfort. Ignorance is a privilege. We live in a time where we must always ask questions.

IGNORANCE. PRIVILEGE. COMFORT.

On my way home from the landfill, I stopped at our local beach, which is my favorite place on Earth. The jet black sand shines so brightly that I always think the stars from last night fell down. It captures my curiosity every time. But this time, I started to notice there was something else in the sand too. Plastic. On this beach. I remember inhaling a sharp deep breath and thinking the trash had followed me all the way from the landfill to my favorite beach.

As I sat down with this revelation creeping up on me, I watched an old man sweep the sand with a broom. His job was to take care of the cleanliness of the beach. He positioned the pile of plastic he had collected away from the wind on the beach, and in one swift movement, he lit the pile on fire. The plastic went up in flames, and I watched, shocked. Hoping it was a mistake. Wanting to trust that it had to be a mistake. He had to know that burning plastic was bad! Not only for his health and the people around us right now, but it was also bad for the environment.

I asked him, "Why are you burning all the trash?!"

And his answer restructured the way I started to think about the plastic problem forever. He stopped sweeping, leaned his body on his broom and, with a shrug of the shoulders and the saddest eyes ever, he looked at me and answered.

"What else am I supposed to do?"

He told me he knew it was bad. He told me he tried to get it picked up, but that there was no effective waste management: no system in place to pick up or sort the plastic and recycle it. There was no system to properly manage it. And the plastic keeps coming to the beach. We keep destroying it. And his job is to keep it clean. So that's what he does.

He knows it's bad. He *knows*.

And he does care. He *cares*.

But what else is he supposed to do?

I had no idea what he was supposed to do. I felt bad for asking. But asking questions where the answers make us uncomfortable is good. I was uncomfortable. The plastic problem was big – much more complicated than I could imagine or even begin to understand.

This moment shaped my path through life and fed the questions burning inside of me. It made me realize that many people ask millions of questions every day. But it's what they do to find the answers and solutions that truly make a lasting impact.

So, I advise you: keep asking questions and keep finding answers. Let your curiosity lead you.

LESSON #7: ROLE MODELS MATTER

Same Diary Entry
29th September, 2012. I was 11 years old.

Dear Diary,

This week was awesome! I did some really cool things and met some cool people. First of all, on Wednesday, I met Nengah, (a girl who competed in the Paralympics doing weight lifting from a wheelchair), and the Soleman, (a man who walks around Bali barefoot to raise money for poor children).

They made me realize that anything is possible, even when you have a low part in your life. I am really proud that I got to meet them. It really was an honor.

Many things happen when you are 12 years old. Especially at school. Especially in that period just before and during middle school. Your first real exams, your first kiss, maybe even your first boyfriend, lots of acne outbreaks, and mood swings. Parent-teacher conferences get pretty serious, classes get harder, and friends come and go.

As we were navigating the ups and downs of middle school, my sister and I started learning about people who had made a real impact throughout history. There is always that time in school when you start learning about inspiring people, like the two examples I shared in my diary entry. Globally, there comes a time when you also learn about the historical work of people like Lady Diana, Nelson Mandela, Martin Luther King, Jr., and Ibu Kartini. We learn about their stories, how they saw a problem in their community, and they actually did something to change it.

Oh, what I would do to hear their stories again for the very first time.

My whole life changed after I learned that people like this existed. It's like it unlocked something inside of me. Suddenly, I had a whole other level of role models to look up to. Before knowing these world changers, we were probably like every other teenager, fanning over One Direction and Justin Bieber and the outfits of Taylor Swift. I think there was even one article I remember hearing about that Taylor Swift's legs were published more times in the media than climate change in an entire year. Let that sink in. Makes you think about our value system, doesn't it? But then again, these celebrities and pop artists were the ones we would look up to because they were all we knew. All we saw. All we talked about with our friends.

You cannot become what you do not know.

I'm glad I learned about changemakers. I'm grateful I got access to these stories of real people doing real things to change the world.

EXAMPLES. STORIES. HISTORY.

My sister and I were obsessed. We watched documentaries, and we dressed up as them at school theme parties. Seeing and hearing about real people who made a difference was empowering. You knew that change was possible. They were the proof of it. But something else stood out to us: the people we were learning about were both dead and made history a long time ago before we were even born.

So although they were inspiring, they did feel far away. Perhaps even a little bit like a fairytale, but then better. My sister and I were determined to make them proud. We wanted to be just like them when we grew up...but we didn't want to wait until we were done with high school or graduated university! We wanted to start right away. We wanted to do something *now*.

LESSON #8: FIND YOUR FOCUS

It was on the couch at home one afternoon after school that my sister and I started brainstorming, our books and color pens sprawled out in front of us. We thought our first goal was to narrow down the challenge we wanted to focus on. The white empty page stared back at us. We started a good old-fashioned mind map with a big circle right in the middle. Inside the circle, we wrote "problems on Bali."

What are the local challenges?

We drew lines out from the circle and wrote problems – anything we could think of went on that list. Luckily, or rather, unfortunately, there were many that came up easily:

Water Crisis + Drought, Air Pollution, Overdevelopment, Traffic, Unhealthy Fast Food Diets, Plastic Pollution, Flooding during Rainy Season, Mosquito Bites, Bali Belly Issues (the world famous tummy problems that tourists get from eating our islands street food), Food Waste, or Stunting (the cause of a Lack of Nutrition).

Actually, Bali had so many challenges that it was hard to stop the list from growing. As much as beauty existed around us, we knew that the reality of these challenges was present too. And it wasn't rocket science. Even at 10 and 12 years old, we saw what was right in front of us. And we saw it for what it was, nothing more, nothing less. Our age might have helped, but there was a level of curiosity that sparked our eagerness to see the beauty, and at the same time, the destruction. Our skies, ocean, rice fields, mountains, and rivers were under threat. Our communities faced one health crisis after another. Making this list felt overwhelming.

We knew we had to focus. So we asked ourselves the second question that anybody starting their changemaking journey should ask:

MIND MAP

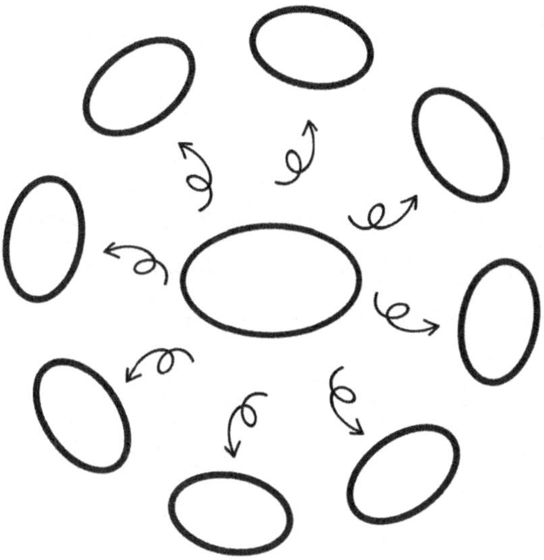

What is the one challenge to focus on?

Once we came up with a nice long list of the challenges, we decided to scratch out the ones that felt least aligned to our passion and skill set. We decided to start off with the things we absolutely *did not* want to focus on. This made the process much easier, but it was still a compromise between the two of us. We had to find something that we both cared about.

I cared about stopping the insane overdevelopment, while Isabel was not so convinced. She's always been a big foodie, so she wanted to do something about food waste. I didn't see a tangible enough project for that focus.

And we also had to find something that fit our abilities. Our experience and skill sets were pretty limited as two little girls. But our imagination was running wild, and we knew we could do something. As the list became smaller and smaller, it came down to addressing the water issue or plastic pollution.

We decided to focus on plastic pollution because it felt more tangible. We could see a clear "before" and "after" result in our heads. And besides, plastic was such an "in-your-face" problem. Everyone could see it. Everyone could feel it. Whereas the water crisis felt harder to illustrate, even though it was just as important.

But again, focus and tangibility, those were the reasons why we chose to stand up for the environment against plastic pollution. At 10 and 12 years old, we already knew that without those two elements, we would go nowhere. We had to walk our talk. We had to set ourselves up for success. So, if we were going to tackle the plastic pollution issue, what were we going to change, *exactly*?

What is the goal, and is it achievable?

Even though we had focused on one topic, plastic pollution, we couldn't help feeling that plastic was still a big issue. We actually used to say in our early speeches: "Plastic is a *big* problem, so we leave it up to the *big* people." So what exactly were we, the little people, going to do about the plastic problem? How did we break down the plastic problem? We learned that 40 countries had banned single use plastic bags. One single use item that countries were saying no to. Even Rwanda has a ban where they didn't let you in the country with a plastic bag! How cool is that?

So, that was how the plastic bag became our tunnel vision focus.

"If they can do it, we can do it too!"

Saying no to single use plastic bags was an achievable goal. We knew it because, just like our individual role models, we now had country role models implementing this change. We had a feeling that if it's been done before in other countries, it means that it's not *impossible.*

That was all that it took.

Bye Bye Plastic Bags (BBPB) started because we didn't want to wait until we were older to start creating change. BBPB was a vision my sister and I had to make our island home of Bali plastic bag free.

We were excited. We were ready. But we were also so naive. Little did we know that what we were about to start would change our lives and our home.

What has worked before? What didn't work, and how can you be different?

We knew this wasn't a revolutionary idea. Like we had discovered, countries had done this before. But what worked and what didn't? Why? This was where we had "homework" for ourselves. And this time, it was homework we actually enjoyed and cared about. We're big believers that you do not have to reinvent the wheel.

Bye Bye Plastic Bags is nothing new. The solution of reducing single use plastic consumption has been around for a long time. Many organizations and individuals have been trying to push for this change long before us: on the island and globally, too.

At the time of brainstorming, there were already many leading and influential voices who had been active for years. Local individuals, expats who had moved here decades ago, government initiatives, and even some company start-ups that were tackling the issue of plastic. My sister and I started our homework, and this is what we observed in the successful implementations:

- Like us, women were mostly at the forefront
- Like us, it was often grassroots efforts
- Like us, it was driven by a fear and worry of drowning under all this plastic
- Like us, these efforts came from a place of good intention

We were inspired by organizations like Eco Bali created by Paola and Ketut, recycling most of Bali's waste through private sector initiatives. They are the most passionate individuals you will ever meet, running a business that many would consider not profitable and not worth your time. But they prevailed to create Bali's most successful private sector recycling facility.

We were excited to hear that the Bali Clean and Green Campaign was up and running, led by the government. This campaign was created in hopes of creating a united front across the island to stand up and make the island "clean and green" once more. It focused on community empowerment and education.

There were up-and-coming programs like Diet Kantong Plastik, a group based out of Jakarta working towards a plastic bag free Indonesia. Then there was Malu Dong, Trash Hero, Surfer Girl – there were so many. And that was so needed!

But what made us different? What could we do to help move this island closer to its goal of less plastic?

We did more homework, and this was the list we came up with:

What made us unique?

- **The timing was right**. After years of campaigning, the island had reached a level of awareness that was never there before. People could see, feel, hear, even taste the plastic everywhere. And they, too, had enough.
- **We were focused**. Instead of overwhelming everyone with the BIG CHANGE we wanted to see, we focused on one, tangible call to action: we were asking everyone to say no to single use plastic bags.
- Last, but definitely not least, **we were a bunch of cute kids leading this movement**. I used to hate saying this was a strength,

because to me I was always slightly disappointed that it took a bunch of cute kids for adults to start taking these problems seriously. We weren't supposed to be doing this.

But it is true when you look back that we started at the right time, we had a focused vision, and we were kids leading the way. These three ingredients made us special. It's what helped build the momentum. Even though it was a slow start.

Still, sitting on the couch, brainstorming, we asked ourselves the next question we knew would come up. We had to focus on our *timeline.*

FOCUS. TIME. ACHIEVABILITY.

LESSON #9: CHANGE TAKES TIME

What's your Timeline?

Naively, we thought we would reach our goal of making Bali plastic bag free by the time summer was over and the school year started. Oh my. When I think back to that moment, how beautiful it was to be that oblivious. We were extremely disappointed when it did not happen in the summer of 2013, and it did not happen again in the summer of 2014 nor 2015. Frustrated was an understatement. But hey, at least we had a goal in mind.

Let's go back to the start. We're back on the couch, with our mind map in front of us. We had found our focus of plastic pollution. It was in the middle of a discussion on what was next that my mum came in with a plate of fresh fruits. It was an after-school snack ritual. Only this time, she saw we weren't doing our homework. She saw our messy mind map and color pens all over the place.

"What crazy plan are you hatching up today, girls?" My mum asked with a knowing smile. My sister and I tried to smile back, but our smiles were strained because we were stuck. How possible was this goal, actually?

Our mum could see the hesitation in our smiles and asked us, "What's wrong, girls?" We unleashed everything at once. We told her our vision of a plastic bag free Bali. We wanted to achieve this specific goal. She patiently looked at us and simply said, "Always work backwards from your goal."

We didn't really understand it at the time, but she unlocked our appreciation for timelines. We had to set ourselves up for success. We started with a goal of banning plastic bags before the summer of 2013 was over. It didn't happen, so we adjusted our timeline and changed it to 2015 instead, giving us more time than we started out with. It didn't happen in 2015 either, so we adjusted our timeline to 2018. It finally happened that year, and was implemented in 2019. But looking back, the power of:

- Having a timeline was key because it gave us focus for an end goal
- Being open to adjusting timelines and letting it empower instead of shut you down if not reached

Change is not linear, it's the exact opposite.

PATIENCE. LEARNING. PLANNING.

Considering all the above, starting is easy. It's actually the easiest part of making something happen…it's just starting. Once you have the courage, have asked the right questions, and have a vision and focus, taking the first step is daunting, yes. But considering the journey ahead, I would argue it is actually the easier part of the journey. I know it's not something you want to hear. Especially not if you're just starting. But it's something I wish someone had told me before.

Starting is easy – to *keep on going* is where all the hard work is!

The work it takes, the energy it requires, the time, the funding, the team you need to keep on going: this is where it gets tough.

I had this realization later on in my journey. This wasn't just a hobby anymore. I'd gone from an inspiring little 12 year old to a full-time changemaker at 22, with a company, office, and team of my own.

This book is filled with real stories, lessons, and loads of questions from more than half of my life. And, for the most part, it's magical, but there are a lot of challenges too, moments where I and the movement wanted to give up, but kept on going.

It's pretty impressive, and I'm still surprised at how far we've come from that brainstorm at home. To be honest, I couldn't imagine doing anything else. And it's all thanks to the curious 12-year-old girl, lifted by her questions, the role models who inspired her, and the support of people around her that shaped her to who she is today: a full-time changemaker.

CHAPTER TWO:

THE PROBLEM & EXCUSES

Lessons in this chapter:

#10: It's worse than we think
#11: Time is ticking
#12: Trust change will happen
#13: Overcome climate Anxiety
#14: Think Big
#15: Don't be fooled by excuses
#16: Share your Knowledge
#17: Speak the language of Data
#18: Adjustments are good
#19: How to navigate community feedback
#20: Inaction is Expensive
#21: Change is the only constant

A poem written in 2014
I was 13 years old

From where I sit,
I can hear a constant click
tick tock tick tock
All is a mystery, only one thing's for sure
My hatred for the clock
With its constant tick tock

When there is a problem, there is always a solution.

Sometimes it's more simple than you think, and sometimes it's quite a journey to get there. But, it is always possible. Even the word "impossible" says "I'm Possible." I know it's cringey, but it is true. Anything is possible, that is the mindset I'm going to ask you to keep before diving into this next chapter. You're going to need it. There will be no sugarcoating it. No fantasy. Just the real, big, bad problem.

LESSON #10: IT'S WORSE THAN WE THINK

Scientists have been telling us for decades now that we are running out of time. The Intergovernmental Panel on Climate Change, mostly known as the IPCC, is an intergovernmental body of the United Nations. Its job is to advance scientific knowledge about climate change caused by human activities. That is the key highlight here: *caused by human activities.*

Now, the IPCC was set up by the World Meteorological Organization and the United Nations Environment Programme in 1988. Its first official report was published in 2013, and today it consists of more than 195 members who are scientists, government officials and experts who contribute their knowledge towards the climate crisis.

What we know:

- The world must rapidly shift away from burning fossil fuels – the number one cause of the climate crisis.
- The global surface temperature was 1.09°C higher in the decade between 2011-2020 than any decade between 1850-1900. The past five years have been the hottest on record since 1850.
- Climate change is caused and accelerated by human activities. But a more accurate narrative should be focused on the fact that, yes, it is human activities, but these are "industrial activities." We know that more than 70% of emissions come from just 100 companies.
- And, even if countries achieved their climate pledges (also known as nationally determined contributions or NDCs), the World Resources Institute finds that they would reduce Green House Gas (GHG) emissions by just 7% from 2019 levels by 2030, in contrast to the 43% decrease we would need to achieve in order to limit temperature rise to 1.5 degrees C.
- And finally, the IPCC shares that there is a more than 50% chance that the global temperature rise will reach or surpass 1.5°C between 2021 and 2040 across studied scenarios, and un-

der a high-emissions pathway, specifically, the world may hit this threshold even sooner – between 2018 and 2037. The global temperature rise in such a carbon-intensive scenario could continue to increase, potentially rising 3.3°C to 5.7°C by 2100. To put this projected amount of warming into perspective, the last time global temperatures exceeded 2.5°C above pre-industrial levels was more than three million years ago.

Many species are reaching limits in their ability to adapt to climate change, and those that cannot adjust fast enough are at risk of extinction. As a result, the distribution of plants and animals across the globe is changing, and the timing of key biological events such as breeding or flowering is altering. These trends are affecting food webs, which results in a changing harvesting schedule which in turn influences the availability of different foods. So we begin to see the "chain reaction" of climate change.

All life on Earth – from ecosystems to human civilization – is vulnerable to a changing climate. There is not a single corner left on Earth that will not be affected by the climate crisis. This is truly a code red for humanity, as stated by the United Nations Secretary General Antonio Guterres.

It's crucial that we all adapt this mindset of understanding how bad it really is. Not to be led by fear, but to be empowered with the facts and science that exist so we can do something to change it. So, read those reports, attend events, listen to a podcast. Anything.

LISTEN. TO. THE. SCIENCE.

LESSON #11: TIME IS TICKING

Time is of the essence. We know we do not have the luxury to wait until we are older to lead by example. Time is ticking.

We feel each moment passing by, and the problem is only getting worse. So here we are: us kids in our campaign shirts, on the streets and on the stages, surrounded by leaders and their excuses. Oh my.

The complicated business of simple change. There I was at 12 years old, thinking that saying no to single use plastic bags was going to be easy peasy lemon squeezy. That quickly changed for me, and saying no to plastic bags started to feel like the hardest goal ever. I almost wanted to give up. The structures of power seemed like a maze that we could not understand.

I learned that saying no to *one* single use plastic item was actually way more complicated than I expected. Why? We learned about systemic change and the spider web of the political world. The complex science and nature of information reaching people. We saw very quickly that our systems think with a traditional, outdated, "stuck in problems only" mentality, which can only result in digging the hole we are already in, much, much deeper.

We learned that the problems of our world are much worse than we think. But because of the ticking clock, we stayed focused on our goal to ban single use plastic bags. And even then, we somehow ended up getting a crash course in:

- What it takes to convince governments
- How to mobilize hundreds of thousands of people

- Finding alternatives to plastic bags
- Creating surveys and citizens' science reports with lots of numbers and data
- Debunking deeply rooted psychological fears towards change

We are constantly learning and adapting
and creating
and inventing
and mobilizing
and organizing
something.

But our goal always stayed crystal clear. From cleanups to social enterprises, school presentations, or government meetings, our goal was to say Bye Bye to plastic bags. We knew what we wanted to achieve: a plastic bag free Bali.

And we were not stopping until it was done.

LESSON #12: TRUST CHANGE WILL HAPPEN

But how long until this vision would be achieved? The knowledge of how bad it really is and the pressure of time has created a generation desperate for change. But do we trust that change will happen? And who will lead it?

One of the major global guidelines created to help reach that vision of a better world is called the 17 Sustainable Development Goals (SDGs).

What are the 17 SDGs?

Created in 2015, the United Nations introduced the 17 Sustainable Development Goals. These goals cover everything from No Poverty (SDG 1) to Quality Education (SDG 4) and Gender Equality (SDG 5) as well as Climate Action (SDG 13). There is a diverse range of goals with the focus on making a more fair, equitable, and sustainable world. The goals target three main pillars: people, planet, prosperity.

It is the global action plan that we are all a part of. If we achieve the SDGs, we would become the first generation to end extreme poverty and reverse the climate crisis.

The deadline of these goals being reached is … drum roll please… the year 2030. That means, in the year of publishing this book, we should be more than halfway there. Yet, science tells us that we have not even reached 15% of these goals. The commitments and leadership of our current systems are not accelerating this change fast enough. This is one of the most dangerous mindsets to take over humanity: a lack of trust.

A real sense of leadership is missing, and after years of scientists telling us that we need drastic change, with little to nothing happening … it is no wonder that 80% of my generation feels a sense of worry towards our future. Sad, isn't it? That nearly our entire generation carries this worry for something that should be so exciting; our future.

TRUST. GOALS. IMPLEMENTATION.

When we cannot see our goals or visions implemented, we begin to lose trust in the systems that lead us. Goals stay goals, unless they are implemented. Without this implementation, a new feeling arises:

Climate Anxiety.

LESSON #13: OVERCOME CLIMATE ANXIETY

Have you ever heard of "climate anxiety"? The first time I heard this term, I felt a click inside. *This* is it. *This* is exactly what I've been feeling my whole life without even knowing what it was. Climate anxiety is directly related to our feelings of stress, overwhelm, fear and grief towards the climate and ecological crisis.

When I was about nine years old, there was a storm one night, and the rains and winds were like never before. Later we found out we had gone through some sort of unprecedented typhoon: the first of its kind in our region. During the storm, we were at home, and our parents woke us up from our sleep. They shook our shoulders until we sat up straight, barely awake but in full panic. The sound of their voices laced with that much worry still rings in my ears.

We saw their anxious faces and climbed out of bed as they rushed us into the living room. We saw branches and leaves scattered around our open living room and the picture frames on our walls had fallen on the floor. The winds were so loud that it sounded like a thousand wolves were howling. It was so scary. "Come on, girls!" It wasn't safe to stay in our living room, so we ran to our kitchen to take cover. It was the farthest away point from all the big trees that surrounded our home. Their big branches scratched our roof, threatening to break down our house. One tree lived inside of our house; it had its own "room" and glass walls around it. I remember peering out from the protection of the kitchen wall that divided us from the living room. The house was a mess. Branches and leaves were scattered across the floor. A chair had toppled over and slid to the other side of the living room. The worst part of it all was the sound of the walls of our house starting to crack. We watched as the walls of our living room started to crumble. I can't remember anymore if it was the house or me, shaking uncontrollably.

This is a reality for so many of us growing up in island communities. Across Indonesia, the extreme weather patterns have scared many of us and have even displaced hundreds of thousands already. Even our capital city, Jakarta, is sinking.

On one of our yearly expeditions through Indonesia, we saw the impacts of the climate crisis up close. First, we had a school presentation on one of the islands we were traveling through for the expedition where 40% of the students didn't show up due to the surrounding floods. The climate crisis was directly impacting how students have access to education. We learned this was a common occurrence during the four months of the year when it rains heavily.

Secondly, we met a lady who lost parts of her home because of the climate crisis. We stumbled across the small shop attached to her house and sat down for lunch. As we ate, I saw how close the ocean was to us. The waves were at the walls of the shop, and as I peered around the corner, I saw something strange.

"It happened last night," I heard a voice behind me say. "The ocean took our bathroom walls," the woman said. I noticed fragments of brick sprayed across the beach. I saw a toilet and a sink at the shoreline as well, three meters from where the foundations of her bathroom were. It dawned on me that not only was this her shop, but this was where she and her family lived.

She told us about how she woke up in the middle of the night to the sounds of the walls tearing apart, the sound of the ocean eating away at her home. She shared her fears about it happening again, and next time taking more than the bathroom.

She told us, every year it gets worse and worse.

CLIMATE. CRISIS. ANXIETY.

Globally the fear of the climate crisis looms on a daily basis. The recent rate of sea level rise has nearly tripled compared with 1901-1971. Homes slipping away into the ocean and floods or flames engulfing entire towns cause more and more of us to become climate refugees. Homelessness, disease, financial instability: this is all interconnected to our changing environment. Another chain reaction we see caused by the climate crisis.

All of this anxiety gives us two options:

1) Feel paralyzed by the humongous task ahead of us
2) Feel empowered to do something about it now in whatever way we can

The majority of the generation I am a part of chooses to use this anxiety as an accelerator for us to keep going. Although there is this worry, a new hum of the hustle begins, and each moment is filled with the beat of:

We must continue. We must do more.

We want change.

Now. Now. Now.

LESSON #14: THINK BIG

What I am about to share is how my sister and I began to truly "think big" – how we channeled our anxiety, frustration, and lack of trust into tangible action. It started with our first experience on an international stage, leading a hunger strike and meeting the governor of Bali.

Our very first international appearance was in India. My sister and I were 11 and 13 years old. We had never been to India before. But we had learned about so much of their history, especially of the changemaker, Mahatma Gandhi. His work as a peaceful activist inspired both my sister and me, and through Mahatma Gandhi we learned about India.

So, of course we were thrilled when we heard that the event INK Talks would be hosted in the very city where Gandhi lived. Little did we know that our visit to India would turn out to be one of the vital moments for our changemaking journey.

When the day finally arrived and the Ink Talks in Mumbai were about to take place, we were ready. My sister and I had rehearsed and rehearsed our speech, memorizing each line. When we walked through the doors of the conference hall, the venue suddenly felt so real and big, and we felt so small.

And we were small. But our vision was big, so we stood behind it and took that stage. It took 15 steps to get up to the middle of the stage. My sister and I turned to each other and nodded to start. We looked out into the audience, but the room was dimmed and the bright lights shined directly into our eyes. We squinted, taking a second to adjust.

I took a deep breath in and started, "Bali, island of gods."

Pause.

My sister continued, "A green paradise."

"Or," I questioned, "a paradise lost."

"Bali, island of garbage."

"365 days ago, we were standing in front of a much smaller audience introducing our initiative to ban plastic bags on our home island. We have been at it for a year now, and we would like to talk to you about our personal journey, the lessons we learned, and a touch of our initiative."

COMMITMENT. DETERMINATION. CHALLENGE.

We were pretty damn proud of ourselves walking off that stage. The crowd cheered and gave us a standing ovation. My sister and I were buzzing. The excitement of the room was contagious. *They heard us.*

As we walked through the crowd of people to our parents, we received a lot of positive feedback. But the first thing we asked was this: "Can we go to Gandhi's house now?"

When we stepped out of the tuk-tuk, a lifelong dream for both my sister and myself was about to come true. Gandhi's house had been turned into a museum – a preserved moment of history. It was a simple home; there weren't many bright colors or loud furniture. There were corners where I would sit and drift into a daydream. I would think about what he was thinking when he was planning something. How would he sit? Where would his mind drift off to?

At the end of the tour, I was silent. I was consumed by inspiration. My mind kept wondering, *What was he thinking*? I wanted to do something. *What would he do?*

Being in Gandhi's house inspired me to go on a hunger strike, just as Mahatma Gandhi had done himself. A peaceful protest that gained the attention of thousands to move towards a better world. My idea was to go on a food strike for as long as it took until the government of Bali agreed to meet with us.

Two weeks after the talk in India, my sister and I had brought up the idea of a hunger strike multiple times. After several consultations with nutritionists and compromising discussions with our parents, we came up with a plan. There is something called a mogok makan in Indonesian, which translates to a fast from sunrise to sunset. That's what we were going to do. We were going to do a mogok makan. No food from sunrise until sunset, every day until the governor of Bali would agree to meet with us.

This news traveled far and fast. As soon as word got out, the story went viral, and radio stations as far as Australia wanted to hear from us. Articles were being written in Europe. The news story about two little sisters going on a food strike traveled the world. But here in Bali, we were yet to hear back.

Our first day of the food strike was on a school day, so we woke up extra early to properly prepare. We ate a small breakfast before the sun came up. Outside, garden lights were still on, and it was so early and quiet in the village. We finished our plates and got ready for school. We felt strong as we waited for the sun to come up. At school, all of our friends and teachers checked in on us every five minutes.

"Are you sure you're okay?"

"Do you need to take a break?"

"Are you sure this is a good idea?"

No, I wanted to say, *I don't know if this is a good idea.* But this was the last chance we were giving the government to take us seriously. By lunchtime, we started to feel light-headed and weak, but we kept on going.

The last two hours of school we were less active and contributing less than usual. Our ride home was quiet and sleepy. When we got home, we laid on the couch, and you could hear our tummies rumble. We lazily looked at each other and smiled. We kept checking the color of the sky to see how far down the sun was. Our parents tried to give us some food and said, "Girls, come on, if you're hungry or not feeling well, just take a bite of this," passing us a plate of fruit or cookies. We pushed it away, determined to successfully complete the mogok makan.

We walked out to our garden, lifted our faces up to the sky, and assessed if we could consider this past sunset. The sky was dark, but there was still a ray of sunshine.

"Just five more minutes," I would say, and Isabel would silently nod her head.

We were on a food strike for 48 hours. My sister and I were at school when our parents called to share that the governor wanted to meet us, and that they were picking us up to go there right away.

I remember being extremely nervous. On the way there, in the car, I wondered out loud, "What are we supposed to say?" and "What if he doesn't agree?"

My mum asked us to look at her. "Girls, you know what to say. You've been working hard for this moment, and it is finally here."

My dad chimed in, "Just be yourself."

I'm not going to lie, in that specific moment, it sounded and felt like the worst advice ever. I didn't know how to handle a massive leader like a governor. I was 13 years old! But I wanted to be taken seriously as a kid on a mission, and we needed his help. We knew we couldn't do it alone.

And then it happened.

The governor walked into the room where we were waiting, and everybody rose to their feet. Isabel and I were the last ones to get up, not knowing that this was protocol.

Governor Mangku Pastika was an old man already, with dyed black hair and heavy, tired eyes. He waved at everyone and told them to sit down. "Please, please, sit, sit," he said, dismissing everyone's obligatory rise to his arrival.

I was told to sit next to the governor in a throne-like chair matching his. I sat with my legs crossed and played with my hands.

He started, "So, you are the girls that are making a problem."

We didn't know how to respond, and then he laughed. It was like a very bad dad joke, and my nerves were frozen solid. My shoulders started to hurt, and I tried to laugh it off too. But then I said, "Actually, Governor, we have something we would like to discuss with you."

Bel and I started a conversation about the plastic problem in

Bali. We presented facts and figures, shared what we were able to do and how so many people from all around the island and the world agreed with us. We asked him what he would do for the mission of Bye Bye Plastic Bags.

He told us, "Girls, you are right."

He told us plastic was a big problem.

He told us he knew he had to do something.

Symbolically, he put on the hat we gave to him, smiled to the camera, and said "Bye Bye Plastic Bags."

Yet, everything and nothing was happening all at once.

We tried to bring the conversation back to a tangible goal. I wanted him to focus on the problem. So I continued, "40 other countries have banned single use plastic bags, and it's shown that this works to reduce the plastic pollution. We think Bali can do this."

He hummed noncommittally, nodding his head in deep thought.

My 13-year-old self waited patiently, not sure what for.

My 13-year-old self wondered how we choose our political leaders.

My 13-year-old self waited still.

He said, "Do you already work with the environmental department of the government?"

I remember being surprised at the strange direction of the conversation. We said no, although we would love to be connected. But I kept wondering, *But sir, what are you going to do?*

He waved at one of his people to come and make a note. He said very strongly, "Make sure these girls meet the head of the environment department as soon as possible, okay?"

My 13-year-old self thought this must be what leaders do. *They delegate, and they distract.*

We told him about how we believe Bali can be a showcase island for Indonesia and the rest of the world against plastic pollution. He said, "Let's do it!" He looked at the Memorandum of Understanding (MOU) that we had prepared and signed it on the spot. He smiled and kept the hat on, said it was a pleasure to meet us, and wished us all the best. He shook our hands, walked out with the hat on his head and the shirt around his arm. We walked out with the signature we wanted, but my hand felt heavy from the feeling of false hope.

It was the first, most bizarre interaction with a real government representative in a high position. Quickly, I learned that this was just the tip of the iceberg and not at all the finish line.

Thinking big can land you a seat next to a governor, but it can also open a Pandora's box of all the new complexities of a world you once had no idea of, like 12-year-old Melati just wanting to make her island home plastic bag free. So simple, or so she thought. Turns out thinking big also requires you to be ready for the big world.

LESSON #15: DON'T BE FOOLED BY EXCUSES

The more we began to interact with politicians and traditional institutions, the more excuses we would hear for why we should *not* change. The most common ones are:

* Excuse: People are not ready for change
* Excuse: There is a lack of knowledge
* Excuse: Change is Expensive
* Excuse: Fear of Change

Ha! Can you believe it? My blood boiled the first time I heard this come up within the walls of a conference. I thought to myself, "They must be joking, right?" I remember even turning to my sister in the chair next to me, eyebrows raised. She looked at me and shook her head. There is no way. We saw the divide as clear as day.

How could they be so oblivious?! How could they be so ignorant?! If only they had seen our action of the world ocean day. Or our annual cleanups, which brought together thousands of people in one day. Or what about the thousands of petition signatures we collected? If only they listened to the communities suffering from the plastic pollution. They could not possibly think that people "outside" the conference walls are not ready. We are right here. We are asking for more change.

"People are not ready for change." This was a hard concept for me to understand; it was the first excuse I would simply not accept.

A man leading the meeting, dressed in a Batik uniform, tried to give me an explanation: "*Iya*, yes, Melati, not everybody is like you. Many people are still not ready for change." As he said this to me, I just looked at this old man's mustache. He pushed the rim of his glasses back up his nose and looked at me as if it was the most obvious thing ever. He looked back up to the rest of the room filled with government leaders, and he concluded the meeting. Just like that, everyone closed their empty notebooks and walked out of the room, taking a free meal on their way out. Food always seemed to be the most important part of these meetings.

As everyone left the room, lunchbox in hand, I remember sitting there going through the options I could think of that created this disconnect and resulted in the first excuse of "people are not ready for change."

1) These political leaders really are clueless
2) There's a lack of interest
3) They benefit from the disconnect

At the end of it all, I came to the conclusion that, it is, in fact, not the people who are not ready for change but it is these traditional institutions that are not ready to change and to challenge their comfort and privilege.

Our vision was simple. But it felt so complicated.

How do we simplify it for our political leaders? How can we show that people are ready for change?

We brought this up one time at a BBPB team meeting and everyone around the table was just as shocked and surprised and disappointed that this was even a topic of discussion. But still, what were we going to do about it? It was time to make some noise.

"Why not organize the island's largest cleanup efforts led by the people? In one single day, thousands of people, from the north to the south and the west and the east, joined together to show that we want a clean Bali."

In 2017, under the people's movement "One Island One Voice" we organized Bali's Biggest Clean Up for the first time. It was a major success. At the start, we had no idea how to organize an event of such magnitude. We had hosted small events and workshops before, but nothing with as big of a goal as this. But that didn't stop us. We worked together with our team and built this vision into reality.

The result surprised us all. There were so many people who were willing to jump on as a coordinator and host their own cleanups! We had structured the model of this event to be a fully volunteer-led cleanup – empowering any individual or group to host their own cleanups on this one day, which eventually became a weekend-long action of cleanups. It worked! Within 6 weeks of planning and coordinating, we had thousands of people joining our event in the first year, from the mountain regions to the beaches all around the coast. We had running clubs that would host cleanups on their trails. Dive groups hosting underwater cleanups. A beach bar would give out free beers or a coconut for each kilo of plastic someone would bring in. Schools gathered for cleanups, musicians hosted cleanup concerts. People showed their strengths and contributed in their own unique ways to this movement.

Bali's Biggest Clean Up became an iconic annual event on the island. We ran it for a successful seven years in a row. Quickly, this day had become one of my favorite days of the year. It beats Christmas and, some years, it even topped my birthday. I LOVED this day because of how our island came together as a community. There was nothing better.

The yearly event hosted by One Island One Voice started with the vision of uniting our communities across the island to host cleanups wherever they are. Over the years, Bali's Biggest Clean Up has cleaned up more than 100 tons of plastic in over 300 locations on the island of Bali, mobilizing more than 70,000 individuals.

Over 70,000 individuals that made noise and said "we are ready for change."

We showed the government that change needed to happen now. But still, we heard different excuses and explanations as to why change couldn't happen faster.

DIVISIONS. EXCUSES. REFUSALS.

The second excuse we would hear is "people don't know any better." But even at 10 and 12 years old, we knew an excuse when we heard one. As they say, with knowledge comes great responsibility. And with that comes my next lesson.

LESSON #16: SHARE YOUR KNOWLEDGE

"People just don't know any better."

Change can start in the classroom. If we learned something new at school, we would dig deeper and begin to understand. We would find connections. With knowledge, we can build bridges.

It was the start of the academic year, and I was entering grade seven. Our new team of Bye Bye Plastic Bags started to prepare for school presentations. We were a group of about 15 kids, including my sister and I. We started to plan what our presentations to other students would look like.

We knew we wanted to open with a question. Something simple

like: is plastic good or bad? Certainly an easy question like this would be motivating for students and allow us to establish what was what. We all knew plastic was bad anyway. The rest of our presentation came together smoothly. We had our why, our what, our how, and we had our call to action for more students to join our team.

By the time I finished writing the scripts, my fingers had blisters and ink all over them. I remember not sleeping well the night before the first presentation. The next morning, I was trying to calm my nerves. I looked in the mirror and said to myself:

"You can do this."

Yet, I was still nervous about the presentation. What if it didn't go well? What if we were late? What if someone forgot what to say?

But we had everything planned out. I like plans, and I like how hard we work to make them. But I'm also a professional overthinker. I took the script off my bedside table and read over it one last time. I splashed some water on my face and looked back up at my reflection.

"I can do this."

My sister and I both wore our campaign shirts, and so did our friends. It made it feel real.

We were on a mission, and we were not alone.

The teacher who had invited us to her class greeted us out front.

"Welcome! The students are so excited to meet you. At our school, we try to teach the students about the environment as much as possible. But it is difficult." She went on to share that it wasn't really part of the curriculum, but some teachers tried their best. "That's why we're so happy to have you!"

We all nodded and kept looking at each other. I knew these shared looks were to let each other know that we were all nervous. I had a good feeling about this though. We had prepared so well.

The teacher opened the classroom door, and chatter erupted from inside. The students were so noisy! I remember thinking how chaotic it felt when we stepped in. It was a traditional Indonesian classroom, with the students all wearing uniforms and posters hung up on the walls. At the front of the classroom, there was a whiteboard, and above it hung the portrait of our president and his vice president. The Indonesian flag and the national symbol of the garuda proudly hung on the wall too.

"Diam semuanya!" the teacher said, which translates to "Silence everyone!"

The teacher's voice cut through the chatter, and suddenly everyone became aware of our presence. Including ourselves. I suddenly felt the intensity of the stares from all the students. *Someone should talk.*

Naturally, my body wanted to hide behind the teacher, or slip off my chair and hide under one of those tables in the classroom. I was not made for talking. It was not my thing. But for whatever reason, I found myself taking the first step in front of the rows of students. I looked back at my friends in their Bye Bye Plastic Bags shirts, and we all got into position.

The teacher opened, "Good morning class, today we have a very special presentation from friends your age! They are on a mission to make Bali plastic bag free. It is a very important topic, so be quiet and listen." I didn't like her tone so much because I wanted them to be inspired to join, not listen just for the sake of listening. And we definitely wanted them to be part of the discussion. I shook it off, and as I looked up, I thought, "*This is where change can start, right here in the classroom.*"

The potential excited me. With a quick nod to my teammates on my left and right, I started with our simple opening question:

"Is plastic good or bad?"

The classroom erupted once more, and students jumped up from their seats. They all raised their hands. They called out, over each other.

Pick me, I know the answer."

"I know it too!"

"Please, please, please, pick me! I know what the answer is!"

"This question is easy!"

Together, the students shouted the answer back to our simple question:

"Plastic is GOOD."

I thought the floor underneath me must have fallen, and I had crashed into an alternate universe. I kept my cool. But this was not in the script. This was not the plan. My sister turned to me, one eyebrow raised, and I knew she was asking me "*What now?*" The rest of the presentation would not make any sense if they believed their own answer of "plastic is good."

Okay. The room fell silent as expectant students looked our way. Out of curiosity, my next question came up. I asked them *why*. Why did they believe plastic was good? And one by one, they offered their explanations:

- **Plastic is good** because I don't have to pay for it (in Indonesia, plastic bags were always given for free)

- **Plastic is good** because I can burn it, and it's gone (a common practice was burning trash – out of sight, out of mind)
- **Plastic is good** because it's easy to use
- **Plastic is good** because toys are made from it

And the list went on and on and on. This was based on their reality. It was something they never talked about. It wasn't something they ever questioned, nor were they ever guided to see things differently. We learned how to shape our presentations and workshops based on this level of awareness. We learned just as much from leading these workshops as students were learning from joining these workshops. Peer-to-peer exchange unlocked so much curiosity, so much potential within us to create change. I know that change can start in the classroom if we are empowered with knowledge.

But change also needs to start in many other rooms, too. From the classrooms to the boardrooms and conference rooms. Decision-making power needs to break away from the conventional disconnected ways and realize that they, too, have a lack of knowledge. It's not just on us kids to learn about these challenges.

This excuse is two-sided. On the one hand, it is true that we don't know enough, and that's where the power of classrooms teaching about climate change can play a big role. But on the other side, what about our leaders? It is easy to hide behind the excuse that there is still too little knowledge or "data."

KNOWLEDGE. CLASSROOMS. AMPLIFICATION.

Sharing your knowledge can look different for everybody; it isn't only restricted to speaking in a classroom. It could also look like sharing information on social media, attending community gatherings, working with local groups, mentoring someone, or volunteering at an organization.

Sharing knowledge is a powerful way to grow in your own learning experience, but also to help amplify and accelerate the learning journey for many others. We all have a responsibility to share our knowledge.

LESSON #17: SPEAK THE LANGUAGE OF DATA

I used to hate the word "data." What more do we want to see? What more proof do we need? Another beach covered in plastic? More birds and turtles and whales washing up dead on the shores? Their tummies lined with plastic debris? The data seemed to be so obvious and right in front of our eyes, yet somehow, it still wasn't clear. Data seemed to be the only thing we needed to convince governments that we needed to change.

Soon after starting Bye Bye Plastic Bags, I realized one of the biggest problems we were facing as a youth-led organization: we weren't speaking the right language. And no, I don't literally mean a language like Indonesian or English. I was speaking a totally different language. I spoke the language of a 12-year-old who cared deeply about the environment and what happened to it. I cared for the trees and the people and the fishes. I cared for everything between the land and seas. It was inspiring, but it wasn't resulting in change happening. I needed to speak the language of data: the language of numbers.

Great, I thought, *I suck in math class already. How am I supposed to speak the language of numbers to politicians who should know more than me?*

Putting myself in the shoes of these linear and traditional thinkers, I started to ask myself a series of questions I never thought I would:

- If we don't change, how much will it cost?
- If we don't vote green, how will that affect the elections?
- What is the cost of a burning landfill vs. the cost of waste management infrastructure?
- Do we reward the good? Or penalize the ones doing harm to nature?
- How much will we earn if we keep our beaches clean?

These were questions that seemed impossible to answer – especially as a 12-year-old. Where did we even start?

Luckily, throughout the entire journey of changemaking, I was surrounded by talented, smart, passionate people. When it came to learning this new language, I thought of Roger, someone who has helped the movement since the very first day. Lucky for us, Roger is all about data.

His organization Making Oceans Plastic Free creates and analyzes surveys and their results. "Knowing where we are now allows us to create a map for the future." I loved how he combined the two languages: love for the environment and the language of data. This seemed to be the perfect formula! Roger soon became a mentor.

Together, we worked on turning one of our biggest annual events, Bali's Biggest Clean Up, into a citizen-led, science collecting opportunity! Suddenly, this wasn't only a successful event to show that people are ready for change; now, we could also use it for useful data collection.

Roger saw a bigger potential for this event: to debunk the excuse that we lack knowledge and data for change. We used Bali's Biggest Clean Up to collect all the data we needed. In a meeting after school with Roger, I remember him explaining what we needed to collect and why.

"The process of collecting data is complicated, but it doesn't have to be!" I was curious to hear what Roger had in mind.

The data collection sheet we created ended up being a really successful and useful tool to help organizations and governments understand what plastic was out there. In this way, speaking the language of data really helped us translate the level of urgency to decision-makers.

DATA. MEASUREMENTS. COST.

After several years collecting this data, we made a lot of adjustments.

LESSON #18: ADJUSTMENTS ARE GOOD

You need to stay positive. Stay strong and aware. I was really proud to be including this citizen science aspect to our cleanups. I really thought it was a good and helpful tool. But others thought differently. In the first year we released the survey, we had a lot of comments from people saying it wasn't comprehensive enough. We would get long emails from our supporters, partners, and random volunteers, saying it didn't have enough detail in it.

So, we adjusted for the next year's cleanup, and we got an influx of messages from people saying it was now *too* detailed and way too complicated to fill in. Our percentage of submissions dropped to an all-time low because people either couldn't be bothered, or they didn't feel they had the skill set needed to complete the survey. So this was a tango dance of its own. Trying to find the perfect balance took a lot of trial and error with a lot of adjustments.

It made me realize that adjustments are a part of the process, and that it requires a lot of patience. Adjustments shouldn't hold you back. Although it was a frustrating experience, it was also my first time learning how to navigate community feedback.

PATIENCE. TRIAL. ERROR.

LESSON #19: HOW TO NAVIGATE COMMUNITY FEEDBACK

When I got all the messages about adjusting the surveys, I made the mistake of taking it personally. For me, this was a hard switch to make – from personal to professional – because it wasn't easy to read the comments or hear feedback that I wasn't doing good enough. But that was the first adjustment I personally had to make: *it wasn't about me.*

At the same time, it isn't easy to feel like all your hard work is being taken the wrong way. I would get so depressed and frustrated that I would write angry poems in my room, hot tears running down my face. For so many years, criticism towards the movement always felt like a personal attack. I would feel a deep punch to my gut every time someone would say something negative about what we were doing, whether it was a constructive comment to our cleanups or team members quitting.

The moral of the story is basically: ***you cannot be everything to everyone.***

Below are five key steps of how I have learned to navigate community feedback to improve the movement:

1) Listen to all sides of the story
2) Always keep an open mind
3) Remember why you started
4) See what adjustments can be made to reach your goal
5) Never lose sight of your goal

Over time, I have learned that I shouldn't take these things personally. Adjustments are necessary because we are constantly learning new things. Our community holds us and our movements accountable. Community feedback will always be an important aspect of changemaking. And understanding how to navigate feedback allows you to stay strong in your vision while still making the necessary adjustments to improve as you continue along your journey.

LISTENING. FEEDBACK. ADJUSTMENTS.

LESSON #20: INACTION IS EXPENSIVE

Every time we would get somewhere with our goal, we would hear this next excuse pop up. “Fine, we have the data,” they would say. “Fine, you proved that people are ready for change. But what about the practicalities? What about the real solutions and the alternatives?”

A general manager from a hotel told us, “Girls, we would love to ban single use plastic bottles and give the guests a reusable bottle instead. But that would cost us a fortune!”

So here we go again with the questions I thought I would never ask:

- What are the budgets for companies to spend on sustainability?
- What are the cost differences between convenience of plastic and relatively new alternatives?

The fact of the matter is that plastic is cheap and easy. Those two reasons are why we still use it on a mass scale today. Many of the alternatives are still too costly in the short term to implement at an industrial level.

And of course, next to the question of costs, there is a question of readiness. We know the alternatives are here. There are plenty of innovations already, mostly in the form of start-ups, driven by passionate grassroots efforts and still operating on a small scale.

Again, there were no connections between these start-up ventures and established businesses. I found it frustrating that, in fact, all the money we need in the world exists. It’s right there! But the willingness to spend right now for something that might not always seem to have instant results is not always there. Systems aren’t in place to support the scalability of some of these innovative products. For example:

Seaweed solution

Seaweed is a magical creation. Not only does it help regulate our oceans and give an immense amount of minerals to our own health, but seaweed can also be a very strong and useful material.

Mushroom solution

Another cool innovation is the mushroom fibers! Scientists have discovered that mushrooms have a strong, fibrous structure that can be used to create many sustainable materials for packaging. Not only that, but it can also act as a substitute for materials in industries of building, food, and clothing!

Banana leaves & Banana Fiber solution

Using banana leaves is nothing new. In fact, before plastic was invented, the Balinese community used banana leaves as their way of wrapping, packing, and transporting products. Today, we see technologies allowing us to extract the banana leaves and tree fiber and turn it into a much stronger material. This is where we see banana fiber being used as a new alternative to plastic.

These are some leading organizations or platforms that you can look to for alternatives to plastic:

Tom ford Plastic Innovation Prize

Tom Ford launched the Tom Ford Plastic Innovation Prize, the only global competition focused on creating scalable and biologically degradable alternatives to traditional, thin film plastic poly bags.

Lonely Whale

Lonely Whale was founded in 2015 and has spearheaded impactful global movements to raise awareness and offer alternatives to problematic plastics. They also convened a consortium of multinational brands to create the first global network of ocean-bound plastic supply chains.

Plastic Pollution Coalition (PPC)

Founded in 2009, Plastic Pollution Coalition is an advocacy group and social movement organization that seeks to reduce plastic pollution.

We know that change is here, and the technology and innovation available today only means that it's a matter of time and political willingness. So yes, we know:

Change can be expensive, but the cost of inaction will be even worse.

We already know how important speaking the language of data is: at the end of the day, numbers are important to convince people to change. According to an article by the Climate Policy Initiative (CPI), they estimate that climate finance needs to ensure global temperatures do not rise above the 1.5°C range from USD 5.4 trillion to USD 11.7 trillion per year until 2030.

To give you an idea, CPI tracked USD 1.3 trillion per year in global climate finance (CPI, 2023). Though this marks the largest volume of such flows to date, nearly double those of 2019 and 2020, we need to increase this amount by at least five-fold annually to get to the first mentioned goals.

If we're still having a hard time understanding how expensive inaction will be, take a look at these numbers:

- Even a temperature rise of 1.5°C is projected to reduce global working hours by 2.2% worldwide by 2030, costing the global economy USD 2.4 trillion (ILO, 2019).
- Climate-related disasters (e.g., hurricanes, floods, wildfires) were responsible for USD 299 billion in economic losses due to damage to assets and capital in 2022 alone (Aon, 2022).

And if we go back to the examples of plastic: according to the World Bank Group's 2024 report, "Blue economy: Oceans, fisheries and coastal economies", the total cost to governments of managing plastic waste between 2021 and 2040 could reach up to USD 670 billion. The cost of inaction for businesses could even potentially reach USD 100 billion over the same time frame.

As you can see, investing to minimize the impact of climate change and plastic pollution is needed and is worth every dollar.

Learning the numbers behind the climate crisis really made

things more confusing for me. Because honestly, what else do they need? As I've said before, I'm not the best with numbers, but even for me these figures were clear enough to prove – once again – that the climate crisis requires some serious investment and attention. I keep questioning why this is not a priority for *all* businesses and governments? If our stories do not shape regulations, then how come these shocking numbers still don't provoke change?

Short-term and long-term priorities are at odds here. Because although it may seem expensive to invest in renewable, sustainable, and circular solutions now, the cost of inaction in the long term will be even worse. Committing to the research and development of alternatives like seaweed or banana fibers should be accelerated with the necessary investments to make these alternatives the new norm. We can all play our part by supporting start-ups and grass-roots organizations who are pioneering this space.

INVEST. FOR. THE. FUTURE.

LESSON #21: CHANGE IS THE ONLY CONSTANT

At the end of it all, there is still one big obstacle, one "excuse." This was always the hardest to overcome because it had nothing to do with numbers, facts, or data. No "thing" we could teach or learn to understand. It is simply the barrier of fear towards change. We have to challenge our own narratives and emotions towards change.

Even though change is the only constant in life, we are all wired to work towards a point where we are comfortable. For example, our current lifestyle has worked for us (to a point), especially for the previous generation like Gen X and the Baby Boomers, who created the big boom within the industrial era. These generations saw an increase in their modern lifestyle, a growth in wealth and health. It was a time where it seemed that everyone benefited from the explosion of opportunity. And maybe, for a time, it did work. But today, it is a fact that our unchallenged and comfortable lifestyle requires the resources of 1.7 planets (Earthovershoot). We are asking more of Earth than it can naturally and regeneratively give.

We're afraid of change, but science tells us that we are using all the Earth's resources every year by July or August. It's called "Earth Overshoot Day." We literally use up all the natural resources that the planet can sustainably regenerate within a year's time frame within seven months of the year. This means that from July to December, we are "borrowing" resources that should be preserved for the future.

It can be hard to actually grasp what that really means. So, to help us understand, why don't we translate this to something more relatable? Something more personal and tangible. Imagine if we compare how we are treating Earth's resources to our personal budget. This would mean that by July, we would have spent all of our money for that year. Oops! How would we survive from July to December? It is exactly the same for our Earth.

Planet Earth regenerates all that we need from her, but at her own pace and time. Our current lifestyle of take, make, and waste has completely lost sight of that natural timeline. We very rarely think about the consequences for our actions, especially not when we are comfortable.

The definition of a comfort zone refers to a psychological state in which an individual feels at ease, in control, and experiences low levels of stress and anxiety. That's basically what being in a comfort zone means. Most of the time, I feel that many people who live in comfort zones forget that they are in a comfort zone in the first place. It's easy not to think about. We tend to stick to what works. We stay comfortable without challenging ourselves or our lifestyle, definitely not questioning nor changing the "way it has always worked."

Within the comfort zone, people feel a sense of familiarity, safety, and security.

Where does this fear of change come from then? I believe it comes from not being able to imagine how much better life can be if we leave where we are now. We stopped imagining. We stopped questioning and growing. We stopped searching for purpose. If we don't show and learn what is possible, we naturally prefer to stay with what is familiar vs. unknown.

FEAR. SOMETHING. NEW.

So, what have all these major excuses throughout my activism taught me?

It leads me to the belief that we need a narrative change. We need to drastically change the way we think. How can we acknowledge the problems, and then actively work around changing our perspective? How can we step out of our anxiety and fear of change to take action?

A problem is an opportunity. A linear system can also be a circular one.

Change is a funny thing. It can seem so daunting for us when we focus on it. But the simple truth is that the only constant in our entire life, every single day, is change. We are literally changing with every breath. Our thoughts change, our chemical levels in our blood is changing, every seven years even our skin changes! Change is always happening for us individually, even when it's out of sight.

But so is the planet. The planet is changing constantly. And no, I don't mean right now with the climate crisis, although that does make my point. But even when we look further back in history, we see that our planet and its climate has gone through so many natural changes already. Look at the ice age and where we are now.

So when it comes to intentional change, why does it seem so much harder? It still baffles me that banning plastic bags took as long as it did. We were involved for six years before there was a law that passed for the ban on single use plastic bags. And it wasn't just us. Before and after us, there have been so many organizations involved and leading the way toward change.

When they say it takes hundreds to make change, they aren't joking. It's true. It took hundreds and thousands of like-minded people, and it took a lot of time, patience, and persistence.

None of us should be this worried about our world. But if not us, then who? And if not now, then when?

CHAPTER THREE:

HOW TO BUILD MOMENTUM

Lessons in this chapter:

#22: Petitions build momentum

#23: Creativity builds momentum

#24: Always have a clear call to action

#25: Fun builds momentum!

#26: Recognize your strengths

#27: Teams build momentum

#28: Titles make a difference

#29: Create a successful workflow

We were truly unstoppable. Once we started Bye Bye Plastic Bags, it took off on its own and had a roller-coaster effect on our lives. It came to a point where nobody could deny anymore that this movement was gaining mad momentum. It was crazy. It felt like it happened overnight. Thousands of people from all over the world started supporting the vision of making Bali plastic bag free.

But it didn't happen overnight, and it certainly was not magic.

Of course, there are things to point to like, "We started at the right time," and "People were ready for change," but there are some elements we learned along the way that taught us how to keep building momentum. Starting is the easiest part. There is always pure excitement at the start. People who are eager to help and have the chance to say, "I was there when it all began."

But the real question is: how do you keep building momentum, and how do you find people that stay when change takes longer?

If you've ever asked those questions, this is the chapter for you.

LESSON #22: PETITIONS BUILD MOMENTUM

One of the very first things my sister and I organized was a petition. We learned that a petition is a public request to do something, most commonly addressed to a government official or public entity. This was a very public way to show our mission was aligned with thousands of people. Not only did it raise awareness, but it also gave people the opportunity to be a part of a bigger cause, slowly building the momentum.

Additionally, petitions are a very tangible way to collect evidence of public opinion, build community, collect data, and influence the decision-making processes, which eventually influence regulations and policy change. When decision-makers recognize the strength of public support through numbers on a petition, for example, they may lean more towards taking real actions to address the concerns raised in the petition.

So, knowing all of this, it seemed like a smart next step and a "no-brainer" to make our petition and have it go viral.

We sat on the couch after school one day with our parents' laptop in front of us. "Bel, let me do it." I said, batting her hands away from the laptop. It was my responsibility as an older sister to do this part.

We spent the whole afternoon setting up our campaign page on Avaaz. There were images we had to drag and drop, copy that we had to write.

As the sun was about to go down, we looked over our fresh campaign page and hit publish. I released a breath and felt three kilos lighter.

I remember that the first thing we did the next morning was run to the laptop to refresh the petition page. As soon as I logged in, I couldn't believe my eyes. Each time I clicked refresh, the petition's total number of signatories went up. And I'm not talking about one or two names; I'm talking about hundreds of names were added each time I refreshed the page. It showed me a live update of the numbers, real people from all over the world adding their names to the petition. People from so many different countries, who knew about Bali or had visited Bali before. They all agreed that the island should be plastic bag free.

There were many Indonesian signatories as well, and they commented "Finally!" and "Yes, let's do something about the plastic problem."

Everybody could see the need. And it seemed that they saw our vision too! People were ready for change.

I turned to my sister and showed her the page. She wiped her eyes two times to make sure she wasn't still dreaming before she turned to me and said, "This is it! The whole world agrees."

It became our new favorite thing to do each morning before school. We would refresh the page, and hundreds of more names would be added to the list.

During lunch break, we would rush to the IT room and turn on a school computer. Our friends crowded over to see what happened when we refreshed the petition page.

Hundreds of more names added.

We took turns, our friends went one by one refreshing the page, taking each other's seats to try it out for themselves.

We couldn't believe our eyes.

The whole world was on our side.

We were not alone.

This petition was the grounds for our vision to carry real credibility. It was the first time that we felt it wasn't just a silly kids project. Bye Bye Plastic Bags became a movement of so many people around the country and the world who stood behind the same vision: an island free of plastic bags. How much more simple could it be?

SIGNATURES. MOMENTUM. PETITIONS.

Petitions are easy to set up and can have a massive impact. By gaining the support of others, it can feed your own belief in your campaign. Using petitions are a great way to get things started and to follow up on your goals.

Our goal for a successful petition meant getting 1 million signatures. Bear in mind, math wasn't my strong suit, and looking back I joke that we probably had no clue how big that number really was. But, we needed that big goal to help us continue building momentum. We had our tool, the petition, but now we needed creativity to reach our very big goal of 1 million signatures.

LESSON #23: CREATIVITY BUILDS MOMENTUM

Where were we going to get 1 million signatures? It had to be someplace with many people passing through. Somewhere we could collect hundreds of signatures in a few hours.

Together with the team of Bye Bye Plastic Bags, we brainstormed a few options, such as the beach, the mall, or schools and universities. But the one place that stood out to us the most was the international airport of Bali.

It was a creative approach to collecting signatures and building momentum. It was something that hadn't been done before on the island. We wanted to target people who had visited the island and experienced the plastic problem firsthand during their stay. It seemed like the most successful route.

Our approach was simple. We decided to write a clear email to the advertising sales executive of the airport. Our email was ambitious and maybe a touch naive.

But we were hopeful and impatient, so unsure of what our first steps should be and not wanting to wait any longer, we marched to the airport to see who we could talk to. We went from conversations with the janitor on the main floor to the assistant manager and finally the advertising sales executive. It was a process to find the right person to help us achieve our goal of collecting signatures at the airport. Finally, after our pitch, which ended with the vision of asking arriving guests: "Welcome to Bali, do you have any plastic bags to declare?" the executive team jumped with joy.

We managed to secure a partnership with the international airport of Bali. Our team of youth changemakers were given access to the departure halls to collect signatures. We created our petition design, printed stacks of paper, and came ready, dressed in our campaign shirts.

It became a weekly event, and we had so much fun. It was also pretty interesting. The airport had a mix of nationalities, and we quickly learned how people from different backgrounds generally responded to us.

In a high-level summary of the tourists' mentality and their reactions, this is what we all agreed on:

- Australians were the loudest to declare their support to the rest of the departure hall and the easiest to sign up
- Russians always wanted a selfie and would tag us on Instagram
- Americans always offered to donate after signing the petition but rarely would actually follow up

- The Dutch and Germans always asked questions and were critical but would eventually sign after we gave them convincing facts about plastic pollution

It felt like a little social experiment where we learned so much about the world and our unique differences. The airport turned out to be such a creative space for us to build that global momentum we were looking for to reach our goal of 1 million signatures.

Through this experience, we learned three key points of how to build momentum using creativity:

- **Stand Out:** Similar to the airport idea, find ways that your movement can do something that hasn't been done before. Dare to be different and do things differently.
- **Show Up:** Go out there and do it! Attend events, conferences, and workshops to network with other changemakers and potential supporters. Show them that you are there!!
- **Spread the Message:** Engage the media and other platforms to spread your message and actions. Create videos and share recaps through impact reports in a fun and creative way.

THINK. OUTSIDE. THE. BOX.

LESSON #24: ALWAYS HAVE A CLEAR CALL TO ACTION

At the end of the day, it never mattered where they were from, as long as they signed the petition. That wasn't always as easy as we expected. There were quite a few people who didn't agree at all. They were quite vocal about it, too. These were the people who would laugh in our face, tell us to dream on, and say we're absolutely ridiculous. "Good luck" we would hear. We had people blame the Indonesian population for how dirty the island was. One person must have been having a really bad day, because they spat in our faces and said:

"I am never coming back to this island until you learn how to clean it up."

That reaction stayed with me for a long time. I still think about it and wonder if the person really never came back to Bali. Why did they think it was our job alone to "clean it up"? People can be so confusing sometimes.

So, how did we ensure our movement didn't become confusing too? Or at least, how did we prevent the team internally from becoming confused by these mixed messages? Great question. It's really important to stay focused, and you can do this by having a clear call to action.

No matter the reactions or feedback we were getting, our call to action stayed the same for any person, regardless of their background. It was simple: sign the petition to help us in our mission to make Bali plastic bag free. They either signed it or didn't, but they knew exactly what we stood for as a movement. That clarity in our communication helped us find the right people who wanted to sign the petition and join the work we were doing.

SIMPLE. CLEAR. COMMUNICATION.

LESSON #25: FUN BUILDS MOMENTUM!

Just have fun. Honestly, this is an underrated lesson. We often hear it, and it's easy to shrug off. But if I had to tell you one thing it boiled down to on how our team kept going and how we built this mad momentum … my answer would be: we had so much FUN.

One of the things we did to keep the airport sessions fun was turn it into a competition. We made it a fun activity to see who could collect the most signatures. It created a healthy environment to encourage each other closer to our goal. Yet, whenever we counted our total amount of signatures, we would always cheer and celebrate our *overall* teamwork. It never really was about the number one winner.

Next to the sessions at the airport, our team would host trash fashion shows, designing outfits from recycled plastic, and then training for the big community catwalk. We would pull together a surf competition, spending the day on the beach surfing and cleaning up plastic at the same time. Entire afternoons were filled with brainstorming and laughing at all our crazy ideas. And then, we would get to work and actually make those crazy ideas happen.

It was work led by love and fun. It was magnetic. Looking back at how much fun we had, it was probably one of the biggest reasons why others wanted to join in too.

We all want to feel like we belong somewhere, whether that's part of a team or movement or country or cause. And through fun and inviting spaces, we can try to find that sense of connection.

BELONGING. LAUGHTER. FUN.

LESSON #26: RECOGNIZE YOUR STRENGTHS

During our sessions at the airport, I started to realize that I was not the best at collecting signatures. Actually, I preferred it if my teammates would be more extroverted and outgoing. It was so much nicer when they would do all the active talking. It's not that I would hide, but I realized this wasn't one of my strengths, and that was okay.

Our success wouldn't have been the same if we didn't stand out, show up, and spread the message. But it also would never have happened if we didn't brainstorm with our dynamic and diverse team. Diversity has become another buzzword though, just like sustainability. What does diversity actually mean, and what does it look like in practice?

According to the Oxford English Dictionary, "diversity" is defined as "the practice or quality of including or involving people from a range of different social and ethnic backgrounds and of different genders, sexual orientations, etc."

Our team was dynamic and very diverse. We had different cultural backgrounds. We were all different ages, genders, and learning styles. We were a group of youths that didn't really make sense if you looked closely, but it worked because of our shared end goal: Bali being plastic bag free.

What was special was that, no matter our differences, we each brought our own strengths to the team.

For example, Mimi and Wilfred were the jokesters of the group, while Noel handled the serious affairs with government representatives. Leander was the team recruiter, and Billy was the team anchor, polar opposites. Lotte and Inca were the best salespeople on the team, whereas Indigo and Aqil were the more creative team members. We made it work, and we needed all of these different skills.

Even when I look at my sister and myself, we couldn't be more different. Isabel is very outgoing and likes rules, so she often sets the boundaries and is vocal about them. She prefers being told what to do and needs to know what the plan is, *exactly*. She has a high social battery and can be the "rallier" of the group with her loud voice and strong presence. But at her core, she is a real peacemaker. On the other hand, I am way too serious for my age. I definitely don't like to be told what to do, and I'm definitely not a rule follower. I'm stubborn and, compared to my sister, I've got a relatively low social battery, but it never gets in the way of doing the things that need to be done. I work hard and can adjust to new situations easily. So you see, we were polar opposites too.

DIVERSITY. OPPOSITES. TOGETHER.

Recognizing our own individual strengths help us understand the unique role we can contribute back to the larger team and movement. It's a win/win scenario when it comes to building successful momentum.

LESSON #27: TEAMS BUILD MOMENTUM

Finding your role and skills is not always clear at the start. For my sister and I, as young founders, it was important to recognize that our team members have different strengths, and we helped identify these strengths by asking them. If they didn't know their strengths yet, we would find it together by trying out different roles. This is where a lot of trial and error comes in. Without a team, we wouldn't have been able to do any of the fun and creative actions. The petition at the airport wouldn't have happened, nor the trash fashion shows or surf competitions.

TEAMS. ROLES. IMPLEMENTATION.

Momentum does not build without a team to bring the ideas to life. One of the ways for each member in the team to take ownership of their roles is to put a title behind it.

LESSON #28: TITLES MAKE A DIFFERENCE

Not so much in the traditional sense, but having a title can empower people to step into their roles. Whether you are a CEO, a start-up founder, or a young changemaker, a title gives you ownership over your work.

Our volunteer team followed this structure, with these titles:

Volunteer Team Structure

Founders

Board members

Team leaders

EDUCATION Team	FUNDRAISING Team	EVENTS Team
- Lead educator	- Sales recruiter	- Lead coordinator
- Facilitators	- Partners recruiter	- Partnership lead

For a moment, let's take a look at the example of the nonprofit organization Make-A-Wish Foundation. This foundation grants the wishes of children with life-threatening medical conditions. Their former CEO, Susan Fenters Lerch, once told employees that they could create their own fun job titles (in addition to their official ones) with the purpose of reflecting "their most important roles and identities in the organization."

She chose "fairy godmother of wishes" for herself, and the chief operating officer went with "minister of dollars and sense." It's actually a pretty fun and simple way to empower people into their roles by giving them something to be proud of.

I was very proud to introduce myself as the founder of Bye Bye Plastic Bags. When we first printed out our business cards, and I saw my name and title, it stirred something in me. I held the card in my hands and smiled as I thought to myself, "*Melati Wijsen: founder. It has a nice ring to it.*"

At 12 years old, "board members" sounded so official. It excited us. We could count on our board members a lot more, because they had the honor of having a higher leadership position (and more important title) within the NGO (non-governmental organization). Our board members earned this, as they committed more time than our non-titled volunteers.

TITLES. OWNERSHIP. PRIDE.

But, at the end of the day, keep in mind that a title is just a title; it's the "get things done" mindset that is the real achievement. A title can make a difference and create a sense of ownership and creativity, but it certainly isn't *everything*. Some people mistake the title as a status and an end goal. But really, especially in the space of changemaking, it's the ones who have a clear understanding of the end goal who will do what it takes to help reach that goal.

LESSON #29: CREATE A SUCCESSFUL WORKFLOW

Aside from the titles, how do we create a successful workflow where everyone feels empowered to take lead in their roles and ensure that the momentum is built? Below, I share a list of my five tips of what I did every month for the team of volunteers:

- **Define clear roles, responsibilities, and deadlines**
Who is doing what? By when? Clarifying within your team about who is part of which team and what their roles are helps clear any confusion.
- **Have one central person communicate to the team at all times**

That was the task of our team leader: one central point of contact to ensure nobody oversteps or is confused about whom to reach out to.

- **Hold a meeting the first Monday of every month**

We've kept it the same for 10 years, to be consistent and not difficult to remember. The last thing you want is a meeting to feel like an added burden to your team.

- **Reflect on past actions and celebrate the next steps**

This was fun to do but also gave us focus. We could see what we accomplished, celebrate our small wins, but then also give attention to other aspects of work that needed it.

- **Set goals for the upcoming month**

Setting new goals within a short time period is actually really useful to stay focused and, at the same time, see tangible goals and work towards them.

GRATITUDE. VOLUNTEERING. WORKFLOW.

Running this volunteer team for the last decade has been one of the greatest honors of my life. I am deeply grateful and touched by the kind and motivated humans who have contributed so much to the movement. Some of my favorite memories are when I think back to those early days of the movement, when my friends and I gathered around a table or added to a whiteboard at school. The dedication everyone gave to this vision, the commitment, the excitement, it made it easier to keep on going.

But, I'd be lying if I said it didn't come without its challenges. Alongside all the above, I know there were more things that I wanted to achieve and simply was not able to do because of my limitations in a team made up of volunteers.

The great thing about volunteers is that they have the flexibility to contribute as much time and energy as they want and can. Yet, that is also its downside. Time after time, when the rhythm of our volunteer team was at its peak, we would lose a team member to something else: a move, university starting, a job being offered.

It happens, and then you have to start all over again. But here's the thing about momentum: once it starts building, it only gets bigger and bigger. And that is what Bye Bye Plastic Bags was becoming. We were truly unstoppable. An island initiative turned into a global youth movement. Carried by volunteers and young board members, it was incredible to see what we could achieve. We used creativity to build that dream momentum and turn a small idea into something much bigger than one person or one organization.

Then vs. now

My idea of a successful team has evolved with my changemaking journey. When I was younger, the sky was the limit. I used to dream of a big office, with many people running around. In my future office, I used to envision a room just for brainstorming, and I would draw sketches and visualize it being an epicenter of my activism.

In reality, here is the evolution of what a successful team looked like:

12-year-old Melati: Happy with her friends and the small team making big change. No office, no set rules or roles, just friends and a clear vision.

15-year-old Melati: Amazed at how big the volunteer team was becoming. A global expansion was happening as well, but she had a vision of one day opening her own office with hundreds of full-time people – that would be success!

19-year-old Melati: Standing at the opening ceremony of her very own office that she built, 15 people on the payroll, having started five active organizations. Was this success?

22-year-old Melati: Learned the hard way that people management and team building was not on her list of strengths.

It's crazy when I look back at that reflection and evolution. As a founder, you give everything you have to the organization – without question. The longer I did this work, the more I realized that it wasn't that way for everyone within the team. Life happens, priorities shift, another better offer comes along, or a career change happens. For some people, a job can sometimes really just be a job. But for me, ever since I started this work, this job was my life.

The saying goes, "Teamwork makes the dream work." And don't get me wrong, I believe it. But when did teamwork become so hard? That was a question I couldn't quite answer.

So, I made finding my dream team my mission; because if you want to build long-lasting momentum, you need a good team.

CHAPTER FOUR:

THE BIG OFFICE & THE BIG TEAM, A DREAM OR A CURSE?

Lessons in this chapter:

#30: Pivot when things aren't working
#31: An office changes everything
#32: Dreams do come true
#33: Take your time, trust your gut
#34: Good ideas travel far
#35-44: 10 lessons on going global
#45: Do the things you want to do
#46: Choose your priorities, mange distractions, & make decisions
#47: No big teams, just the right people
#48: You cannot do it alone

Along my journey with Bye Bye Plastic Bags, I've had the privilege of speaking to more than 1 million young people around the world. While on these adventures, I noticed something inside of me was bubbling … I felt something missing. There was a bigger dream growing: YOUTHTOPIA.

A vision was materializing: one that realized our generation needed a place to come together and just be. A place where we could learn and exchange ideas. I wanted to create a platform that I wish had existed when I had started my changemaking journey, a platform that brought together the tools, community, and network to scale important work even more. But also, it would serve as a platform to simply find incredible humans.

When Bye Bye Plastic Bags finally achieved its ban on single use plastic bags in Bali, I started to give more attention to this growing vision. Unlike BBPB, which started off from an adventure of following questions and a touch of childlike obliviousness, I wanted to start this next project "right". Whatever that meant.

I was older than when I started BBPB, I wasn't 12 years old anymore, I was 18 and freshly graduated. I thought I should come up with a business plan. It didn't work out. In fact, the first business plan was a major fail, and a really expensive one at that. It had involved a brand new coded platform, but we had put a paywall in front of our educational materials which did not work for our target audience: youth. Overall, it took three teams across India & Indonesia to build the first-ever prototype platform of YOUTHTOPIA.

I tried so hard to do what I thought I had to, forgetting how and why I actually do this impactful work. After months of no revenue, and the vision being held back by the pressure of a "business model,"

I decided to pivot. It clearly wasn't working, and I felt that the reason was because I wasn't holding true to my vision of creating an accessible learning platform for anyone to join.

LESSON #30: PIVOT WHEN THINGS AREN'T WORKING

Today, YOUTHTOPIA is a free learning platform that hosts hundreds of ready-to-go, studio-produced programs where young changemakers share how they made an impact. We got rid of the "code from scratch" idea and used something readily available as well. There was no need to invent and code something that already existed. That wasn't our goal, anyway.

YOUTHTOPIA is unique in itself. Essentially, all our programs are a blueprint for the many different ways to create change. Masterclasses, workshops, mentorship, grants: these are some of the offerings YOUTHTOPIA has on its learning platform – all for free, because we want to answer that frequently asked question of:

Where do I start, and how do I keep going?

At YOUTHTOPIA, we are hundreds of young changemakers with our own projects and track record of change, coming together to share best practices and ideas. We believe in community-powered solutions, we practice transparent and clear communication, and often give honest feedback and peer review.

If you want to join our community and start learning from young changemakers, check out YOUTHTOPIA with the QR-code on the next page.

ALIGNMENT. EMPOWERMENT. PLATFORM.

When things aren't working, instead of shutting down, let yourself explore what the root cause is. Use that as motivation to remind yourself of your WHY. Oftentimes, things aren't working because we stray from our purpose. Naturally, things stop aligning. Find the courage to admit it, and pivot.

There was a shift when I changed my model of teamwork from a volunteer team to a full-time, paid team with official titles, contracts, job descriptions, and their own desks in the brand new office.

The shift from a volunteer mindset, ready and willing to jump in where needed to a "it's not in my job description" of paid team members was so drastic, and nobody prepared me for that.

I went into building a team with a Hollywood version of what it would be like.

Headline: *"Grassroots activists make a global impact on education and youth empowerment from their brand new, upcycled container headquarters."*

Um, I wish.

It didn't really occur to me that there would be a difference between volunteers and a full-time team. The only thing I thought would change would be the availability of people. Nobody would leave for university or hop to the next island to catch better waves midway through a campaign. I didn't expect a change in attitudes, expectations, and demands. And I was definitely not prepared for what running a full-time team would do to me personally at 18 years old.

At the start, I was eager to get a full-time team in place, because after four years of only volunteers with Bye Bye Plastic Bags, I was looking forward to being able to count on people to complete the tasks, from start to implementation. Volunteers are amazing, and we definitely wouldn't have built the momentum we did without them, but it was also always tricky to plan ahead.

Good communication was everything; the last thing you want with a volunteer team is:

- Confusion in their tasks and responsibilities
- They misrepresent your cause because they don't really understand its mission
- They start something without finishing it because priorities and expectations were not translated clearly

For the first four years of BBPB, the only people working "full time" were myself, my sister, and my mum, who helped in the background. There was also always an additional person or two who supported tremendously at different points in the campaign, on a volunteer or part time basis. And even then, my sister and I had school, and we were technically full-time students. My mum had her own company that she built. And the people that were so kind to be there and support more hands-on were doing it mostly from the good of their heart. On top of it all, we certainly didn't have the funds to be able to give someone a full-time salary. But we all made it work and aligned with beautiful humans who saw the same end goal as us.

But let's get this straight: a handful of people running the operations of a massive global NGO with 30+ teams and an average yearly calendar of over 130 events is a mission in itself. At the time, BBPB had 30-100 volunteers of students from schools all over Bali. It was impressive. We had turned one room at home into our little "studio" that hosted one table and a wall full of images of our activism throughout the years.

When I finally finished school and could focus full time on Bye Bye Plastic Bags, and later YOUTHTOPIA, I decided I wanted a full-time team that would help me grow the organization to the next level.

GROWTH. CAREER. SERIOUSNESS.

LESSON #31: AN OFFICE CHANGES EVERYTHING

I was convinced that after years of having no "real" office, the first step to achieving my goal of a full-time team was to build an HQ.

Before we had our own office, every meeting would be at the nearest cafe to our house, just outside of our village. Warung El Passo was an open-air cafe with lots of plants around the tables. We loved it. The local Balinese team at the cafe soon felt like an extended part of our team. Every monthly meeting was hosted there, every new partner was signed there, every email was sent there, thanks to their Wi-Fi. It was unofficially our office space.

But it didn't *feel* like our office. It was a cafe. There were other guests using the space, mostly nomads (it is Bali, after all). It was loud, and on most days, sticky and hot from the humid air (again, it's Bali). The cafe wasn't an experience that showcased our hard work. We didn't have our projects showcased on the walls, and we didn't have a brainstorm room or a "think" bubble.

If we weren't at the cafe, we were at the BaliOn offices. BaliOn is the name of the company my mum started on the island of Bali focused on property management. She started her company from scratch in our living room, half of it split to be our playroom, the other half her office. One side of the room had our dolls, our drawings, and a big wooden playhouse, while the other had Mum's piles of documents and a big, old-fashioned computer.

When half a room was no longer enough space, Dad built a small wooden room in the garden as a sort of "studio space." The building was simple and humble but cozy, with its glass windows and wooden roof. Mum put desks and cupboards inside, and it started to turn into a real office. She built an entire company from there. She had a logo, printed business cards, and had her first sign put up in front of the gates outside our house. When we were growing up, every other night after putting us to bed, I remember hearing the sounds of my mum opening the door to her office. She worked really hard and put a lot of effort into her business.

When her team became too big for that tiny wooden studio, she got a new, two-story office. One day, she told me she felt proud of her new office, but mostly because she finally had a place to leave her work at the end of the day; it didn't follow her home anymore.

I really felt that. I felt it as a daughter, but I also felt it as a founder myself.

So when I finally had the time after high school when my full-time team was forming, I decided that it was time to build our very own office for Bye Bye Plastic Bags and the new project of YOUTHTOPIA. I needed a place to leave work at the end of the day, so it didn't follow me home anymore.

The vision came to me at the dinner table at home. I was with my family, and they asked me what my dream office would look like. I pulled out the papers and pens we always have on the table for exactly this purpose, for when a dream pops up and needs to be birthed on paper.

Together with my family, we brainstormed what the office should look like and how it should work. I wanted it to stand out and be something different: recycled shipping containers lifted off the ground, a large garden, and the entire property solar-powered.

The final vision for our HQ consisted of five containers, each one for a different purpose: a container for all teams to work in, one container would be divided up with a kitchen and showroom, one would be a meeting room, one would be a think bubble, and finally, one would be my office.

Suddenly, at 18 years old, with no experience in construction at all, we began building my dream HQ down the road from my childhood home. I had to instruct where I wanted things like lights, plugs, desks, and windows. Throughout this process, my mum helped me out a lot. She considered where things had to go: where the big desks and cupboards should go, who would sit where, which rooms could host different events. She helped me make my dream a reality.

My dad taught me a lot about structure and how buildings were made. As we had two containers stacked on top of each other, we had to build stairs. I think my dad was trying to have a hands-on-learning-experience-from-dad-to-daughter moment, as he let me experiment with the steps. When the stairs were finished, I raced up, looked back down, and saw my dad smiling. But I was disappointed, "They're too steep!"

He said, "They're okay, you just have to go slowly."

Slowly. I never was good at doing things slowly. To this day, maybe that's the lesson I think was passed along. I think about the two stairs at the headquarters as "The Slow Stairs."

After many months of construction, my dream office had finally come to life. It felt like a visual representation of everything that we still had to do, but at the same time, it was also a mark of everything we have already achieved. It was a new home, to hold space for all things old and new.

VISION. HEADQUARTERS. BUILDING.

Having an office changed everything for us as an organization. It made us more credible. It took us out of the "passion project" category. Suddenly, partners and funders and even our own growing team saw how this was turning into something serious. The transformation was beginning.

LESSON #32: DREAMS DO COME TRUE

In 2020, on a drizzly afternoon in the middle of the rainy season, we finally hosted our opening ceremony. Partners from all over the island had traveled to our little village HQ. We had the head of police, the local mayor, and media joining us to officially "cut the ribbon."

Despite the rain and the busy end-of-year period, I was shocked that so many people turned up for this milestone. We were reaching our ten years of campaigning and had gathered the support of so many within the community.

My dream of a changemaker's HQ was coming true. We built the headquarters, and now it was time to build the right team. I wish we learned this earlier in life, but building a team for a start-up is hard work. The culture of start-ups is definitely not for everyone, and that's okay. One thing is for sure, though: building the right team takes time.

GO. FOR. IT.

LESSON #33: TAKE YOUR TIME, TRUST YOUR GUT

"Taking our time" isn't something that comes naturally to many of us in the rushed, fast-paced, young changemakers' world. But this was a lesson I learned the hard (and long) way. When you are building your team, taking your time to ensure you are aligned with your new teammates will prevent a short working relationship. The longer I've been doing this, the more I hear it from other changemakers, too! Or anyone building a team, really.

Taking our time during the interview process is important because this is where you set your foundation. Teams build momentum, remember? But not just *any* team can achieve this: strong, focused, aligned teams do.

To build this kind of team, one of the first things to be clear on is your structure of operations. What are you? Are you building a team for a nonprofit? A social enterprise? For-profit? Even if you are just starting out with an idea or school project, you need a team to transform your ideas. And clarity on this structure helps establish a filter for who "applies" or joins the team in the first place.

I believe in multiple interviews and conversations with the same person, as well as introducing them to other existing team members. The first and second interviews can sometimes be drastically different, and getting the honest opinions from existing team members is important.

There are two things I always ask (and ask for) during the interviews:

- "If I called your previous employer and asked them to describe you, what would they tell me?" It's interesting to hear how people describe themselves from someone else's perspective.
- A reference letter: this gives insight to their past professional experiences and puts real people behind their written track record.

Hiring people didn't always go well for me. But over time, we learned to take our time during the hiring process and trust our guts. I have learned to ask the right questions, but also to receive the right questions, as they can say so much about a person. Examples I love to hear asked from an interviewee are:

- "What types of skills is the team missing that you're looking to fill with a new member?"
- "What's the most important thing I should accomplish in the first 90 days?"
- "Can you tell me about the team I'll be working with?"

These questions tell me that people are truly interested and motivated to start working with us and want to do a good job.

Over the years, so many wonderful people joined our full-time team, filling our HQ and amplifying our impact.

JOBS. ROUTINE. TRADITION.

LESSON #34: GOOD IDEAS TRAVEL FAR

We weren't only growing in our Bali HQ. We were growing as a movement, reaching all corners of the world. People from everywhere started to see what we were doing on our island. They watched our videos on social media and immediately reached out. We got emails, DMs, and mentions in comment sections. It was one request after the other: can we start a team in other cities and countries?

I must have been 13 or 14 years old when the first requests came in. It made me giddy with excitement. This was confirmation that what we were doing was important, and even though I didn't know the word then, I knew it was *scalable*. I had my first encounter with scale when Bye Bye Plastic Bags turned from an "island" movement to a global movement. This was different from organizing our island-wide cleanups. Yes, those were pretty big and scaled a lot in their own right. But coordinating events and teams in other countries was an entirely different task. It required so much, and yet it was so simple. It was so clear to me.

In one weekend I finished the first-ever "handbook" of BBPB. I remember running out to the living room with my laptop and proudly presenting the handbook. It had already begun to get dark outside, so I asked my family to crowd around my glowing laptop screen. I remember feeling so proud. It had everything you needed to know and have before starting your own team. It created clarity and set a common foundation for our growing movement.

What was inside the global handbook?

- How to present BBPB, complete with the vision, mission, and history
- Team structure and how to find your supporters
- Logo and how to create it, following brand guidelines
- Action ideas
- The do's and don'ts

This handbook changed over the years, with expertise from many adding to it – allowing it to become the best handbook ever! But this first implementation gave me so much strength in believing that we could actually scale. I knew that multiplying our movement around the world and growing our team would help accelerate the change we want to see.

So, I wrapped my head around it. *Okay, this is happening. We're going global.*

SIMPLICITY. GUIDANCE. STRATEGY.

10 Lessons I learned for a successful global campaign:

- **#35 CREATE AN APPLICATION PROCESS TO START A TEAM:** Don't make it too complicated or too long, but definitely enough so it becomes a filter. You do not want people with a short-term mindset or the wrong intentions (i.e., "It'll look good on my college application") joining your team. Make this application welcoming for all to start, but thorough enough that only the committed ones will finish it. On average, our application took two weeks to finish, as it combined a set of different tasks.
- **#36 ENSURE THE SUPPORT SYSTEM:** It is important for long-term sustainability that your new chapter's team leader has a support system already in place. This can look different for each team. What we usually look for is that they either had support from a) their school i.e., a teacher or a school club, b) their parents, c) at least three other people who would help them.
- **#37 ONBOARDING PROCESS:** Consider this a little welcoming phase, where you get to know each other. Start with

some easy tasks first, like making sure you have all the information of the local team, logo creation, a first action, etc.

- **#38 HAVE ONE POINT OF CONTACT:** In our case, we had a dedicated person for this role, called a global coordinator. This helps keep communication streams clear and also signals your level of commitment to the growing team.
- **#39 EMPHASIZE THE MOVEMENT'S END GOAL AND STICK TO IT:** Our strength was our focus on plastic bags. The minute that our global teams started to promote or talk about other issues, we usually had a sit down with them. Of course we know and feel that the world is struggling through a lot, but focus is what allows our movements to reach their goals. And ours was to say no to plastic bags.
- **#40 BRANDING IS MORE IMPORTANT THAN YOU THINK:** Logos alignment is key to building recognition as a movement. Our logos being so easy to replicate really helped with this. But branding is also important in terms of how you show up in a space, such as wearing your campaign shirts, presenting with the same slides, etc.
- **#41 MONTHLY MEETINGS:** Similar to our in-person team meetings in Bali, we recognized the importance of having consistent meetings with all of our global team leaders. These meetings would happen virtually and act as a space for debriefs, catch ups, questions to HQ, etc. It was a nice way to build community and find like-minded youth.
- **#42 ONGOING COMMUNICATION:** Setting up channels like WhatsApp groups or one-on-one get-togethers was essential and, again, the role of our global coordinator. It's a more

informal way to communicate rather than the monthly meetings, which are a little more structured with an agenda.

- **#43 ALIGN THE EVENTS AND ACTIONS:** As a global movement, it is important to show up in solidarity. We had a few events on our calendar that all global teams were required to take part in, like World Ocean Day, World Cleanup Day, etc. It's also a fun way to get everyone involved and active, creating a positive culture within the movement.
- **#44 THE HANDOVER PROCESS:** Like any healthy vision, the handover from one "leader" to another has to be done smoothly. It's not realistic to expect that your team leader, who in our case was still in school, would continue this work forever. So setting up a clear, transparent handover process is vital for the long-term sustainability

SCALE. GLOBAL. MISSION.

We quickly spread from Bali to 60 locations all around the world. It all happened so quickly and so *well.* The global team leaders were all incredible. They became the foundation for my hope for youth-led movements and their scalability.

But scale isn't everything. Even though we live in a world that tells us *more, more, more* is a good thing, I actually felt that it became harder, the bigger we grew. With a big team and a brand new office, it wasn't a hobby anymore. This wasn't some passion project. This was real.

Where it went wrong

In the height of my hiring, firing, resigning process, I hired around 35 people. And I received 20 resignation letters … in one year.

To put it plainly, that's an insane turnover rate. This was one of the biggest causes of my burnout. I didn't know what I was doing wrong, and I quickly learned that leading a team was not my strength and didn't fuel my passion. Our good and simple idea turned big and messy and complicated real fast. I was accommodating too much of what others wanted from our changemakers' HQ.

I started losing the vision of 12-year-old Melati because I started to become the office police instead of the dreamer. It was not working out the way I had always planned. Projects started but never finished, campaigns were put on hold because deadlines were constantly pushed. I turned very bitter and jaded and started to hate the very job I had built for myself.

The headquarters started to become a place I would try to avoid as much as possible. Can you believe it? The very office that I had worked so hard to build to be a home for the movement, suddenly became a symbol of something I couldn't stand anymore. It made me sad.

So how did I get here? What could I have done differently?

LESSON #45: DO THE THINGS YOU WANT TO DO…

…and not because others tell you it's what you are supposed to do. One of the examples when I think back to that tipping point is the introduction of Standard Operational Procedure (SOP). It might sound silly, but this is the story of how I fell into the trap of doing something because I thought I had to do it.

I never used SOPs in my office. Traditionally, SOPs are created by the HR departments of companies to create guidelines and set expectations for employees to follow. *Rules.* I don't like rules. Certainly not when they are telling you the most basic things like: what to wear to the office, how to welcome guests to the office, what to say and what not to say to students during a presentation. All of this seemed obvious to me. I had learned all of this by doing. I figured it out at 12 years old. The idea of a written, black and white SOP book seemed ridiculous. It wasn't anything that required a certain level of genius or politeness or human-to-human understanding that an average person didn't have. I couldn't wrap my head around why people felt the need for SOPs.

But then I thought of my sister. Despite her incredibly bright personality, her feedback in the workplace has often been that she needs to be more proactive. She tells me, "If I don't have the rules, I can only be active to a certain level."

So, I thought, it couldn't hurt. Why not? People have different needs to perform best. We were growing, and perhaps we would have a few people who needed rules to thrive. And in true start-up fashion, we didn't have a massive HR department to write out our SOPs for us. So, my mum, along with my second lead at the time, made the effort to write and implement what the SOPs would be. It took weeks and multiple meetings and case-by-case scenarios. They both put a lot of effort, time, and attention into it. The belief was that although we were still relatively a small team, we needed the guidance and HR method of SOPs to thrive.

The result was a thick stack plopped down on my desk with nearly 40 SOPs. I was shocked. I didn't know how to react. I kept telling myself, *This is what real companies do, Melati.*

Obviously this was what we had to do. SOPs were the norm.

This is what companies do, Melati.

Those first few weeks with the SOPs felt like fresh New Year's resolutions. You're excited. You think back to it. You reference it. But over time, somehow they became distant papers that didn't do anything. Before I knew it, we were back to the same challenges of not following deadlines, communication with partners slacking, etc.

People told me I needed an HR consultant, which I again couldn't wrap my head around because my team was never bigger than 15 people at once. I had a gut feeling, and instead of honing in on it, I let myself be guided down a path that I knew wasn't where I wanted the company to go. And although it was an insightful distraction that taught me a lot, I learned my lesson to stick to what I want to do, because it's what I want, not because it is what other people tell me to do. Doing things because you're expected to do them won't bring lasting change; it has to come from a place of you *wanting* to do it.

INTENTION. PERSEVERANCE. FILTER.

But of course, there were some other factors that played into this frustration too.

I traveled so much, and that made it harder to run the operations. Obviously. So that resulted in me starting to hire even more people.

Then, I hired too many people for simple tasks. Somehow, I was convinced that the tasks I had been doing as a 12-year-old with a handful of volunteers were enough to fill out so many more full-time, paid roles.

My gut feeling started to form an answer: I wasn't clear in my priorities.

LESSON #46: CHOOSE YOUR PRIORITIES, MANAGE DISTRACTIONS, & MAKE DECISIONS

Things went wrong because I didn't have my priorities straight. A year ago, I would not have been able to say that so easily. But looking back, the lesson I learned during this process was to prioritize.

I admit, the combo of being a teenager and running a headquarters is not the most obvious or popular mix. But it was my reality, and I learned a big lesson when things weren't going right: it was all about how I chose my priorities. It was up to me to make changes. Did I want to focus on a global workshop tour? Or did I want to build an HQ and strong team? Instead of making a decision, I let myself get distracted. I said yes too much. Yes to everything but building a strong team. I multitasked – which, let's be real, doesn't work. Instead, we should be promoting more of a monotask culture: the act of doing one thing at one moment and doing it well with focus, intention, and everything you've got.

I multitasked everyone's job, doing the work for them instead of teaching them the how. I was a "headless chicken running around" (someone once described me as such – a wonderful image of exactly what I was like during this time).

The lesson on managing distractions doesn't mean we can never do things that aren't work-related or try something new. It just means to be open and try new things without losing your focus. Take the SOPs as an example. I learned something new, but I knew it wasn't a part of the vision I was building.

To really tie in the lesson on priorities and distraction, here is a quote that I often think about:

> *"A focused fool can accomplish more than a distracted genius." –Alex Hormozi*

Hold on to that original vision at all costs. And sometimes, I know it's the scary part … that means we have to make decisions.

The older I get, the more I understand this lesson and how important it really is. Making decisions is hard and sometimes a bit uncomfortable. It is way easier to hide behind distraction and a "headless chicken" personality. To me, making decisions feels very out of my comfort zone and is something I am still learning a lot about.

In the past, before making a decision, I would often jump to the next thing and hope everyone forgot about the topic at hand. So, essentially, I would just not make a decision and hope all would be well.

William James said, "No decision is, in itself, a decision." And you can bet I felt the brunt of that "no decision" aftermath when everything was going wrong.

I learned that in order to find the right priorities, I had to actively make decisions. Every day, all the time, I had to make decisions.

What did I want to give my time and attention to? What did the company need right now? Did I want that meeting at 11 a.m. or 11:30 a.m.? The sinks at the HQ were leaking, what should we do? The printer is broken, do we really need to fix it? How much would we set our grants (the grants with which we financially support young changemakers) to this year, $1000 or $1500? Can we post this blog on the website?

Yes. No. Maybe.

Each became a full sentence. It made me empowered and a lunatic at the same time. There were so many moments where I just wanted someone else to make the decision for me. I soon realized that making decisions was the line between a dream and a curse.

EXECUTE. LEAD. CONSIDER.

When I made the decision to start making decisions, it was a game changer. I scheduled days where I would tackle a to-do list of all the things I had been avoiding: my "I really don't want to handle this" list. And one by one, I started to tick things off. Suddenly, really daunting decisions, big or small, didn't seem that difficult. One thing that I think really helped was removing the idea of there being a "right" decision. My focus was to just make a decision. What would come next, we would figure out when we'd get there. I just had to decide.

It actually became really motivating, and I started to feel so good!

Next thing you knew, I was an expert decision maker. Just kidding. We're still getting there. But the thing I am most proud of is making the decision to make a decision.

In the end, I had to remember why I was doing this work in the first place. I wanted to create positive change in my community.

As a young founder, I got distracted often, my priorities changed every now and then, and it took me a while to learn how to make decisions. I learned so much when I was building the team. One of the biggest changes in my mindset was when I decided to change my definition of what a successful office and team looked like.

When I started this dream, it looked like a massive team buzzing around the HQ. But through my experiences, I decided that contributing to this movement looked different for all of us. It doesn't always mean joining a team full time. I've worked with amazing freelancers, part-time contractors, creatives, volunteers, and changemakers.

The team I was building was one big community made up of well-intentioned humans.

LESSON #47: NO BIG TEAMS, JUST THE RIGHT PEOPLE

After taking our time in the interview process, and ensuring our priorities were aligned and our focus was sharp without any distractions, new alliances started to form. When you've gone through all the lessons in this chapter, you start to realize that you've created space to allow the right people to find you. Sometimes, it's being at the right place at the right time, with the right intention for you to find the right people.

LESSON #48: YOU CANNOT DO IT ALONE

With our new headquarters and the community team growing, there was a moment where I sat back and looked at how far we'd come. Nothing I did was without the help of so many members of our team. We really did build a dream together.

I liked that our movement was finally entering another level. We built momentum for years and turned our volunteer team into a full-time team. We moved from a village café to our own headquarters. Finally, it began to feel like we got to enjoy the journey.

TEAM. WORK. REALITY.

Everybody who gravitated to the HQ, whether they stayed or not, at one point believed in the same vision with everything they had. They saw it too because they believed in our story. This is where I learned to never underestimate the power of a good story to change the world.

Bali, 2012: 10 & 12 year old Isabel & Melati during one of their first campaigns on Bye Bye Plastic Bags. We looked at the camera and asked "What are we going to do about the plastic problem?"

Bali, 2013: One of our first official team photos, taken right after a monthly meeting on monday after school. We were so proud of our new campaign shirts.

London, 2014: My sister and I, standing on the red dot of TED. Here we are closing our speech, moments before receiving a standing ovation. All I remember is turning to my sister and giving her a hug.

Bali, 2014: We had just finished our first ever meeting with the governor of Bali after the success of our food strike. Here we proudly hold the signed MOU between BBPB and the government of Bali.

Bali, 2014: With my hero and role model Jane Goodall when she visited Bali. We had the honour of meeting her and talking to her. The work and her story have inspired me to keep on going for years.

Switzerland, 2022: Together with Christiana Figueres at a climate conference. I remember listening to her speak and my smile grew as I thought: finally, a leader that speaks truth to power.

Bali, 2023: Community is at the centre of our work and we often hosted gatherings in the capital city of Denpasar, Bali. In front of government buildings, parks, the streets, our team of youth would raise their voices!

Amsterdam, 2023: Before opening for President Barack Obama in the Ziggo Dome in Amsterdam, I had the honour of meeting him and got to take this photo, a powerful back to back.

CHAPTER FIVE:

STORIES & THE POWER OF LISTENING

Lessons in this chapter:

#49: Exercise your imagination
#50: Never underestimate the power of a good story
#51: Two ears, one mouth for a reason
#52: Public Speaking is a skill you can learn
#53: A good story has many ingredients
#54: Know Your Audience
#55: Change your narrative, not your goal
#56: Focus on your WHY
#57: If the story is there, everything else will follow
#58: Translating stories into income
#59: Sharing opportunities with others sparks joy
#60: Inspiration is where change begins

"A good storyteller makes you want to listen; a great storyteller makes you want to take action." – Unknown

LESSON #49: EXERCISE YOUR IMAGINATION

When we were very small, our parents would take turns putting us to bed. After a long family dinner where my sister and I would retell all the events of our day, we would hop in the shower and get ready for bed. Either my mum or my dad would sit in between me and my sister and tell us a story.

Sometimes they would have a book on their lap and read out loud. Sometimes they would make up a story off the top of their heads.

They were tales of magic and mischief, love, and forgiveness.

It was the best part of the day. We loved it, especially when they made up a story on the spot – the anticipation of not knowing what would happen next! The shock and joy we would have when something unexpected would happen! And then, of course, the smile and heavy eyes we would feel at the end of a story when everything worked out.

"The end" always felt like the best exhale.

CHILDHOOD. WONDER. IMAGINATION.

This is an important lesson because stories are powerful tools to shape who we are. They grow our imagination. We would be nowhere without our imagination.

LESSON #50: NEVER UNDERESTIMATE THE POWER OF A GOOD STORY

Stories teach us how to be creative and guide us how to dream. If imagination were a sport, then storytelling is the activity. Stories also hold lessons passed through time and create a space for us to exchange thoughts, feelings, and so much more.

When I think back to the stories that really shaped who I am, I think back to the lessons at school that we had about people who made an impact throughout history. I can still remember the bubbling excitement when I first heard their stories: Nelson Mandela, Lady Diana, Mahatma Gandhi. Their stories changed something deep within me and made me take action. Without those stories, I would not be who I am today.

INSPIRATION. ACTION. IDENTITY.

LESSON #51: TWO EARS, ONE MOUTH FOR A REASON

A good story teaches us many things. It can also be a powerful tool that teaches us how to listen. Listening is as important as speaking, or arguably, more important. It is said that we have two ears and one mouth for a reason. Being an active listener is not something we learn or practice often these days. Think about it. When was the last time you had a genuine interaction where you were sharing something about your day or how you were feeling or a cool idea you had, and where you felt the person in front of you was actually listening? Like *really* hearing you?

There is a concept of listening that I learned from an indigenous youth leader, Janali Doncaster. We were in the studio one day recording a YOUTHTOPIA Masterclass on the importance of preserving languages. "Language is identity. For us indigenous people, one of our languages dies every 14 days." I was shocked to learn this and couldn't believe what he was telling me.

He explained to me, "We have forgotten how to dediri. It's a term we use for listening. But," he paused, finding the right words, "it doesn't translate exactly to the English word for listening. In English, listening is something you can do just through hearing sound. For us, dediri is listening, but not only with your ears. It is where you listen with your ears but also with your heart and your eyes and your entire soul. This is what listening used to be."

Ever since then, I have wanted to dediri for every conversation. It changed the way I want to consume stories and show up for the people around me.

But of course, sometimes (most times) I still find myself struggling to be a good and active listener. Dediri is hard, takes intention, and needs you to be super mindful and present during the conversation. As a public speaker, it is normal that you start to anticipate what to say next onstage. The stage is an intimidating place to be, and it's not always the most natural position to be in, with hundreds, or sometimes thousands, of eyes staring at you.

I was 16 years old the first time someone used the word "diplomatic" to describe me. Me? At 16? Diplomatic? I had just come off a stage where I was in conversation with someone. We were talking about the work we do and some of the big campaigns we had coming up. The audience was not too big, and the session wasn't that long. But I remember I went up there with an agenda. I had a clear list of bullet points I wanted to share. It was an opportunity for me to recruit new team members, promote our next island-wide cleanup, and call for donations, which allowed us to keep doing the work we were doing.

The questions that were directed to me didn't allow me to share that specific message. So, instead of answering their questions, I went for a walk. I use this expression because it's what I feel like I do onstage sometimes. No, it's not a literal walk. I didn't walk offstage, but instead of answering their questions directly, I took charge of the path of conversation. I would first acknowledge and respond with a sentence usually related to whatever they gave me, and then continue where I wanted to go in the first place.

There used to be this idea in my head where I could blame the other person for asking the same boring, old questions. In reality, I got tired of hearing the same questions over and over again, and honestly, I was also trying new things and answering what I wanted. It took me a while to recognize that at one point, I just stopped answering the questions entirely. I stopped listening. And yes, I do believe there was a time in my life where I entered a few spaces as a little diplomat on my high horse.

I became really good at going for walks onstage.

LESSON #52: PUBLIC SPEAKING IS A SKILL YOU CAN LEARN

Believe it or not, when I was younger, I hated to speak in public. Today, I love it and have made it my career. Public speaking is an art that you can learn. You don't always have to be born a natural. Public speaking is a skill you can learn, develop, and improve every time you do it!

But trust me, I was definitely not the confident natural speaker you see today. Oh no, no, no. Before starting my activism, every time I was asked to speak in front of an audience, whether it be for a class presentation or at a big family gathering, my knees would shake and my palms started sweating. Oh and the butterflies? I had a whole zoo inside of me.

When I started Bye Bye Plastic Bags, I knew that there would be public speaking involved, but it didn't matter. I had found something that I believed in. It felt like a lifeboat in a big sea of problems, so I wanted to shout from the top of my lungs to help more people see it.

Here's the thing: I was shy about speaking in public because I didn't know what I stood for. What was little Melati supposed to say? But then, when BBPB started, it wasn't about me. That was the best part. My introverted self got so excited about this "bigger than us" potential: this bigger story and solution.

Intention makes a good story. What is your goal when you speak up? Because Bye Bye Plastic Bags started from a place of good and pure intention to make my island home of Bali free of plastic bags, the stories flowed easily out of me.

SPEAK. FROM. THE. HEART.

Vividly, I started to see the different stories. Many of our first stories tried to revolve around questions:

- What will happen if Bali drowns in plastic?
- What world do we want to live in?
- How can we change the world?
- How can we unlearn and practice traditional ways of life like Tri Hita Karana?

> *Someone once told me that we grow in the direction of the questions we ask and the stories we tell. It made me think of how stories are seeds: they plant ideas and water our imaginations to grow.*

Public speaking is a skill. It is one of the most important skills to have as a changemaker. Through public speaking and effective and impactful storytelling, I believe we can change and shape culture. Just like how the stories my parents told us when we were kids shaped me, I believe the stories changemakers share can change the world.

5 of the strangest moments speaking in public, and what they taught me

1) Stumbling onstage at the UN

The UN was on my vision board for a really long time. I grew up wanting to be secretary general one day. At 15 years old, I found myself for the first time in New York at the United Nations HQ. A dream come true moment. But we were not as prepared for this speech at the United Nations General Assembly as our previous speaking engagements. We kept reworking the speech because we felt too intimidated by the opportunity to address all these world leaders in one room. Where do you even start?

The night before, we sat on the floor furiously writing down notes and ripping up pieces of paper. Then the morning finally came around, and it was time to go to the UN. The security process itself was already really nerve-racking. The building was surreal. When we saw the signs and arrows pointing in the direction of "UNITED NATIONS GENERAL ASSEMBLY HALL," we felt the real nerves kicking in. Backstage, we could not sit still, and by the time we got called up, we had all this energy circling around our little bodies.

I walked up the stairs first, the bright, shining lights opening up the beautiful hall – this sacred place I had envisioned in my dreams for so long; this powerful center of countries of the world. Behind me, I hear a thud. I look back, and my sister is on the floor. Bel had missed a step and nearly face-planted into the podium. She looked up at me with the biggest smile, and we both burst into a laugh. Quickly, we pulled ourselves together again, but looking back at that moment, we really needed that laugh. It was the moment we needed to break the ice for ourselves.

The lesson: It reminded us not to take things too seriously. We delivered our message, received our applause, and then got back to work. And that was the story of what we learned when we spoke at the UN.

2) The opening line

It was onstage at our TEDxLausanneWomen talk. My sister and I walked up to the little red dot and looked out at the audience seated in the big, beautiful Swiss theater. We took a deep breath in before starting and then … nothing happened. We forgot the opening line. It was Bel's sentence, but I had been so focused on my cue that I actually forgot the sentence too. The room was quiet. We looked at each other. Someone yelled out, "You got this, girls!" and cheered, sending the whole room into applause and loud encouragement to let us know we got this. I got goosebumps and almost wanted to cry.

We looked at each other nervously, and the first sentence came to me. I leaned over to my sister and whispered it in her ear. She repeated it confidently out loud, I heard my cue, and the rest was a piece of cake. The whole story flowed out of us. What we learned after our talk was that because the mic was attached to my cheek by a headset, everyone could hear me whisper to my sister with the first sentence. Luckily, it turned out it was a hit! People came up to us and said they loved our talk, but they especially found our beginning endearing and *"so human."*

The lesson: 1) Remember the full story, not just the cue.

2) Always remember the opening line, and the rest will follow.
3) The audience has no clue what you are going to say, so don't stress too much about it and share the story, whether you remember the planned first sentence or not.

3) You *can* do it

We've been on multiple stages with multiple setbacks: a hangover, a fever, a broken foot, a sprained wrist. We've experienced them all. For the better or worse, we've grown up on many of these platforms, and we took our coming-of-age bumps and bruises along with us.

When I broke my foot, the conference organizers were so kind and changed the stage setup, so that I had a high stool to lean on. When I had a bit of a sore throat after recovering from a cold, I brought a warm tea onstage and would take sips throughout the session. When I had a hangover, I'd clear my day afterwards or cue more videos during the speech. We got very creative.

The lesson: Everything is possible.

4) You *cannot* do it

The hardest stages I had to speak on weren't the ones where we were sick or hungover, not even the ones with a broken foot! The hardest stages I've ever had to speak on were the stages where I had a broken heart. My first-ever breakup took more than a year to recover from. I lost 10 kilos, I didn't sleep, and I couldn't hold a conversation where I didn't bawl my eyes out at some random point. I was a hot mess. And I was in the middle of one of my biggest career moments.

Where the previous lesson was everything is possible, here I learned that sometimes you have to know when you have to step back. There is a powerful transfer of emotions when you tell a story in public. People feel what you feel. And although I could show up and hold these spaces, it was an immense struggle. I was barely holding myself together, and people could see it reflected in my stories.

I cried when someone said, “You’re so inspiring. I want to be like you.” It was a nightmare. People could definitely feel my deep sadness, even if they had no idea what I was personally going through.

The lesson (and reminder): Don’t judge a book by its cover.

5) Condoms to tell the story!

We were on a four-day shoot with a documentary crew, and we saw the most ridiculous thing. We were on day three, shooting an ocean scene. My sister and I were going to go a little bit into the ocean and run out as quickly as possible. We had to do this multiple times while saying something like, “Come on Bali, we can do this.” When we went in to get mic’d up, my sister and I saw that the crew had covered our mics with condoms. We must have been 13 or 14 years old at the time, and we found it to be the funniest thing ever.

The crew explained to us that the condoms were the perfect fit to protect the microphones from getting any saltwater on them! I still remember the moment of discovery.

The lesson: Sometimes to get the story across, no matter the environment, you find (creative) ways to make it work.

The content of the story itself is about 80% of the power. I know from experience that there are a few other ingredients that either make the story land in its full power or just slightly off.

The 55/38/7 Formula

In a 1967 study, it was Albert Mehrabian, a researcher of body language, who first broke down the components of a face-to-face conversation. He found that communication is 55% nonverbal, 38% vocal, and 7% words only.

> I know what you must be thinking - how is that possible? is it true that less than 10% of what you're saying is important to getting the message across?

While there are some corrections and acknowledgements to be made when it comes to the study of the 55/38/7 formula, it does give us a good foundation.

LESSON #53: A GOOD STORY HAS MANY INGREDIENTS

- The structure of the story
- The delivery, including tone and pauses
- Facial expressions and other visual support, i.e., slides
- Our body language
- And the call to action

So many different elements add up to a captivating story and delivery. These five "ingredients" were focal points for me when I started working on improving my public speaking skills.

If we look back at the bedtime stories and traditional fairy tales, they follow a story structure that has been used for generations. Most of the time, the plot follows a model called Freytag's Pyramid, which consists of an introduction, rising action, climax, falling action, and resolution. We focus on the "rising action" of a good story because this creates excitement and tension. If we look at the overall structure, this simply means the plot begins with a problem or challenge, and the main character must act in response to that problem. The problem is solved, the bad people are gone, and they all live happily ever after. The end. *sigh of relief.* It's a psychological formula on what works to get people's attention and keep it.

FORMULA. PREDICTABILITY. GENERATIONS.

I wonder how our story with the climate crisis looming will end. *Cue the main character energy* We are the ones who will save us. People power!

A successful structure

Another thing I've learned is to always implement the practices of the Communication Diamond in all my speeches. One night at home, our mum, who believes that communication is the success or destroyer of everything, told us about this tool. After dinner, we cleared the table, and she brought out the pens and paper we always had ready for learning sessions like this. She started, "Girls, remember that communication is everything. It can help you only if you understand how to structure your thinking. This is what we call a Communication Diamond."

She drew a diamond shape on the blank piece of paper and divided the diamond into five parts. "Think of a story split into five parts. Each section of the diamond is a part of the story, okay?" Within each part, she started writing down the title. At the top of the diamond, she wrote an ice breaker, below that she wrote an introduction, and it was followed by the main message, summary, and finally, call to action.

That is the structure of a good story. A good story can mobilize entire communities around the world. Students who would hear the story of Bye Bye Plastic Bags and what we were able to do in

COMMUNICATION DIAMOND

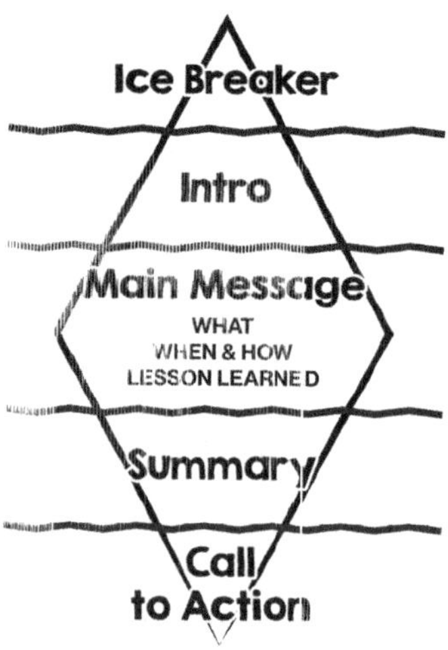

Bali suddenly wanted to do the same. They saw themselves in our story. That is the impact of a good story. It is an invitation. It is a guide.

Ice breaker: This always has to be interactive and fun. Short and sweet. We always used a breathing exercise for the audience for two main reasons. a) It was a way to ground ourselves onstage and get rid of the nervous butterflies in our tummies. b) It was a powerful reminder to the audience that every second breath comes from the ocean.

Introduction: Who are you? What are your project goals, in summary? What will your audience learn from you?

Main Message: Explain how you will achieve your goal. The what, the when, and (we always included) the lessons learned.

Summary: Imagine you are wrapping up a bow on a present, making the finishing touches to your speech. Summarize your main points.

Call to Action: An audience never likes to be left on a cliffhanger. Give them something to do! For us, it was always clear actions like: 1) Say no to plastic bags 2) Join our team 3) Sign our petition. Find your clear call to action.

Keep It Short & Simple (K.I.S.S.)

Next to learning about the diamond structure, we also implement KISS. I always say, "Don't forget to KISS!" in my public speaking workshops to middle schoolers. It always gets them to laugh, which is good, because then they'll remember it.

We are from the TikTok generation. Our attention span is already spread thin, and content is already considered long if it passes 30 seconds. But we can learn from this success formula and apply it to traditional public speaking. We want to capture attention at the same time as delivering a message that stays with our audience.

Which brings me to my next lesson and final point:

LESSON #54: KNOW YOUR AUDIENCE

Preparing to share a story takes time and skill, and it needs intention. But you also need to know who your audience is. Think about it like this: how would you describe sustainability to a group of six-year-olds? And what about to a group of CEOs? Or how about delivering a story on the importance of taking action to a bunch of middle school students, and then to a United Nations task force? There are ways that you can adapt your speech to ensure it comes across to the audience. This makes the audience feel special and seen by the storyteller; it makes the story more impactful and will more likely land in a way that sparks inspiration.

Some audiences will also react differently to your story and message. It won't always be received how you expect – sometimes for the better, like when you receive a standing ovation. My sister and I never expected a standing ovation. The first few times we received one, my sister and I were shocked. The audience, mostly parents with tears in their eyes and hands over their hearts, seemed shocked too, as they jumped out of their seats and erupted in applause. We spoke from our hearts, and it was received by the audience in a positive way.

But it can also go differently, and the reaction you expected doesn't come, like a joke you thought was definitely going to get a laugh. About 60% of the time, my jokes don't land. I'm just not funny like that. Or the moments where you thought, *Fuck yeah, that was a good speech, tons of questions for sure…* but then the Q&A part is so quiet that the MC makes an even more awkward joke than the one you made: "Come on guys, she doesn't bite…"

As awkward as they can be, Q&A sessions after the presentation are also some of my favorite moments. They are pure interaction with your audience, your community, your peers. But they also don't always live up to expectations. The difference in reaction of Q&A lies also in the age of your audience, at least from my personal experience. When I finish a session with younger years like grades 3, 4, or 5, everyone is full of energy. It's hard to describe, and honestly, you leave the room feeling so excited. The curiosity and the questions! Some totally not related to anything:

"What's your favorite color?"

"Do you have a dog?"

"How did you move to Bali?"

All these firecracker questions, one after the other, until the teacher interrupts, "Alright kids, remember, questions about Melati's work. Who has any questions about her project?"

And the group would erupt, shooting their hands high up, begging to be chosen. Some just blurt their questions out because they're too excited.

"What do you do with all the plastic after a cleanup?"

"Why did you only do plastic bags?"

"Is it hard to keep going?"

These conversations and interactions are like food for my soul. It is a reflection moment, where I become honest and open onstage, and sometimes (most times), I surprise myself.

And then, you move on to the older age groups: grades 6–8, the middle schoolers. All of them are way too cool for school, but really, they're still curious about everything. I felt it when I was that age, and now, especially when I talk to middle school students, there is a big divide in this age group. The too-cool-to-care vs. the care-too-much. Traditionally, you could say it's the popular kids vs. the other kids, but I think our generation is experiencing a much stronger social divide influenced by what is happening in the real world. More on this later.

I would finish a presentation to a group of middle schoolers, and the teacher would say, "Alright students, who has a question for Melati? Remember to keep it on topic." But this reminder was pointless, because nobody dared to ask the first question. It would be so awkward I'd want to run off the stage. Instead, I would talk a little bit more about something random for a few minutes to break the ice. The first hand would shyly go up and a small voice would ask the first question, something safe, something easy:

"What inspired you?"

"What was a big challenge for you?"

How did you start?"

These questions, solely because of the fact that it was the first question, I would always overstate how great the question was. "That's a really good question!" "Oh I love this question." "Thank you for asking this…what was your name?"

That brave student would then double check. *"Me?"* they would mouth, and I would say "Yes, what was your name?" They would find the microphone and say their name.

"Thank you, Lily. Shall we give a round of applause to Lily for the first question?" The room would cheer. The ice was broken. And after my answer, tons of hands went up with more questions than we had time for. Huh, turns out it *is* cool to care. I love when we start to realize this in life.

High school students are the most challenging but rewarding audience. Sometimes I get the most anxious and nervous talking to highschoolers and I even find myself feeling like I am back in high school. I know it's funny and maybe even weird, but I've talked to many audiences – and I stand my ground when I say high school students are the most intimidating. So critical and opinionated. So entitled and curious. Honestly, the fastest group to make up and change their mind all at once. It's always a turbulent time onstage, and it's the audience that requires the most attention if you want the most impact.

The sleeping ones in the back, I see you! Sneaky looks on your phone? I see that too. High school students are a harsh audience, and it can feel like they really don't care. But, high school students are also the age group that surprised me the most.

Q&As with high schoolers were the worst. It would take ages, even longer than middle school sessions, and there have even been moments where not a single question was asked. The room was quiet and true to this confusing time in life. Some students were even bold enough to snicker. It made me want to disappear. But here's the thing: this audience is terrified of speaking in group settings. So, as soon as the students were dismissed for a break before the next class or talk, a line would grow. Students lined up, refusing to go to the next class before asking their questions. The questions started flowing like a waterfall, and so many high school students showed their potential.

Naturally, we are curious beings, but through age and especially our education system, that curiosity dies. It is not valued anymore. Anyway, this was the most surprising thing about this audience: despite not wanting to ask questions in group settings, their individual curiosity shone through after the presentation. Showing us how important one on one attention and care really is in the world of education and empowerment.

One day, after a three-hour workshop, a student came up to me. I was wiping the whiteboard clean and packing my backpack when she approached me. Even though I was exhausted, thirsty, and ready to go home and lock up my voice for the next few hours, I could tell she was shy. So, I stopped what I was doing and gave her my full attention. And I'm glad I did, because she asked a question that I didn't feel like I could give a good enough answer to.

She asked, "Um, but how do you do it? How do you talk to friends about this? Because my friends don't care. Every time I try to talk about our environment, or bring your own bag or even something as small as composting, they tell me to shut up or roll their eyes, and it's not always very nice."

No. No, it's not. I almost wish I hadn't turned toward here and had kept cleaning the whiteboard behind me. This question is the hardest. Because this is talking about public speaking to your friends, to intimate circles about topics they may not understand or agree with. There is a lot to say here, but to stay on the topic of knowing your audience, this is how I responded: "I know it's not always easy. I go through that sometimes with my friends too. But try to learn from their reactions. Find out what it is they care about, what makes them excited, and connect it to your message. It doesn't always have to be serious, but you do have to know your audience and invite them!"

ADAPTATION. AUDIENCE. ENGAGEMENT.

Stories are impactful, but without changing your narrative according to your audience, they might not make as big of an impact as they can. Knowing your audience is a key element for successful delivery of public speaking. So dig deep! Find out their age, backgrounds, culture, upbringing, values. This all factors into how they will receive your message.

LESSON #55: CHANGE YOUR NARRATIVE, NOT YOUR GOAL

Knowing your audience is key because you adapt your narrative. But remember, changing our narrative doesn't mean changing our goal. People sometimes mix them up.

For example, the goal is to make Bali plastic bag free. To a surfer, the narrative would relate more to the environment, like: "Let's say no to plastic bags to keep our oceans clean."

To a student, the narrative might have more of a youth empowerment angle, like: "Anything is possible when we work together as a team. Let's make Bali plastic bag free."

To a CEO, the narrative might be more around the business appeal: "Saying no to single use plastic bags will signal to your customers that you're taking sustainability seriously."

ATTENTION. PIVOT. MESSAGE.

Changing our narratives can be tricky because sometimes we lose sight of the end goal or our call to action, which then creates confusion and a lack of consistency. Try to always remain clear with one goal, no matter your audience or the narrative switch.

Remember, it's not about you. I'll say this multiple times throughout my book because I think it's a narrative we need to celebrate more and more in the world of activism. It's not about *you*. In so many ways, you are the messenger. At least, that's how I feel most of the time when I talk onstage.

LESSON #56: FOCUS ON YOUR WHY

There are many of us who spend time onstage to get famous, but that source of motivation is definitely a cause for burnout. It will get you fast and soon. It's not enough fuel to keep going for ten years because your *why* is off. We should tell stories to inspire something bigger than ourselves, to help others imagine something they couldn't see before. Simon Sinek brings this out perfectly in his TED talk on the importance of your why. He believes that great leaders always start with their *why*.

Sinek decoded how great leaders like Martin Luther King, Jr. or brands like Apple have so much success in growing their movement. He calls this formula "the golden circle." He draws three circles in-

THE GOLDEN CIRCLE

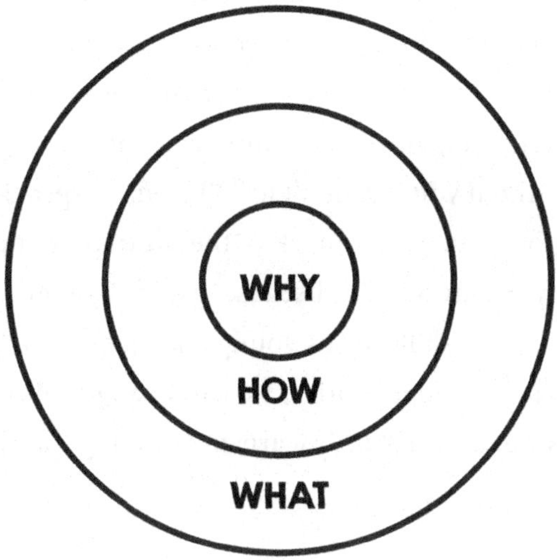

side of each other. The outer ring is the "what," the second circle is the "how," and the inner circle has "why" written in the center.

He explains that 100% of the time, when people explain what they do, they know how to explain it. You know *what* you do. I work for the environment, I speak in public, I have a business in this industry or that industry. Some people know how to explain their "how," but very few people know *why* they do what they do.

"People don't buy what you do, they buy why you do it."

WHY. REASONING. GROWTH.

At the end of the day, do the right things for the right reasons. Speak from the heart. Tell us *why* we should care. There are so many things (mostly cringeworthy advice) that I could share with you at this moment. Hopefully through some of the stories you've heard from me already, you can learn from my experience. From knowing your audience to knowing your why, there's already a lot there for you to unpack. After ten years of speaking professionally, I can say that I still learn something new after every session.

So for now, let's dig into some more of the practical tips for public speaking. And if you still don't feel like public speaking and storytelling is for you, you can skip the next part; but I highly recommend you stay with us because, again, I believe it is one of the most important skills for us young changemakers. We are storytellers because through stories, we can change culture. And the good thing is we can constantly learn and develop this skill. So here it goes:

Memorizing your speech

- Try it with funny accents. My sister and I would crack up every time we did this exercise. It's a fun way to remember what you are saying by hearing your voice in different ways than normal.
- Write it down! The practice of not speaking but writing has helped me loads! I am a very visual learner. If I can see it in front of me, I remember. Literally the act of writing it down by hand makes memorizing the speech so much easier.
- Understanding the bullet point structure of the overall message. This one is important because even if you can't memorize the story you wrote word for word, you need to at least know the body of the message.
- Try it with different audiences: your family, teachers or friends at school.

What to include in a slideshow presentation

- Striking images that tell you the story with no words.
- Avoid too many words or long sentences.
- Be creative, use audio and visuals to support your story, and allow your audience to imagine with you.

You know that saying that people often tell you when you're preparing a speech: "practice makes perfect"? **This is the biggest lie.** Practice does not make perfect. It is very rare that you leave an audience thinking, "Oh wow, that was the most perfect speech I've heard in my life." Perfection is a constant illusion that is hovering over our heads. At least, the idea of it hangs heavily over mine. The worst part about being told that when you "practice you will be perfect" is that it leaves you with two feelings if the speech doesn't go as planned – which, remember, often happens:

- The feeling you didn't practice enough (even though you might have practiced too much already) – cue the start of a hamster wheel.
- The feeling you aren't good enough, and public speaking isn't for you because it wasn't perfect and didn't go as you practiced

BUT this is the problem. What is the solution? Again, we must change our narratives. Practice does not make perfect, but it certainly does make improvement. We build on our techniques, and we get better every time we share a story. When you share a story again and again, you will own it more. You will get better every time you tell the story. This is good! This is what we need: safe environments and opportunities to express ourselves and to exchange with one another.

Learn from your mistakes

For most of us, the fear of starting and the possibility of making a mistake prevents us from even trying to develop our public speaking skills in the first place. It's a fact that more people are afraid to speak in front of a crowd than to jump out of an airplane. Be honest, how many times have you wanted to do something, but then stopped because you were afraid you would fail? Whether it's jumping out of an airplane or speaking in front of a large crowd, I know that fear has stopped me from doing many things in my life. Even with things like trying out for a dance competition or going on solo trips.

We care so much about what other people think. When we keep going, we find the center of ourselves and become so much more aware of what needs to be done vs. caring about how others see us. We find something beautiful. We find who we are meant to be and the stories we care about.

In a documentary I watched about skywalkers, they said this striking quote about what circus performers remind themselves of before their stage time:

"Our full potential is on the other side of fear."

LESSON #57: IF THE STORY IS THERE, EVERYTHING ELSE WILL FOLLOW

When I was 14 years old, I met Flore Vasseur. She was a film director from France who reached out with an interesting story. Her youngest son Sam had asked her what she was doing to protect our dying planet. "Mama, there are so many young people who are doing their work to make the planet a better place," he said one day after watching our TED Talk. He continued, "But what are you doing?"

She was shocked at the question, surprised that this meant so much to her son, who was six years old at the time. Flore started to brainstorm what she could do. Her strength as a storyteller was to help bring out the stories of others from around the world. So, in 2015, she came to Bali to help tell our story of Bye Bye Plastic Bags. It featured in a 90-minute long documentary about the work we do published by ARTE in their TED series.

Flore was one of the first journalists and storytellers that I felt truly heard us. She listened, and she shared. It was the perfect combination where I felt supported and mentored. We would travel from one place to another to show her our work on the ground. Flore had so much energy; she could even match the energy of my 14-year-old self. She was quick on her feet and often took the camera in her own hands to capture the authentic, raw moments.

I loved that about her way of storytelling. "This is the way of a documentary, Melati," she told me one day as we were in the car, just after a cleanup. "Nothing is scripted, and you do your best to capture the truth." I was instantly hooked, fascinated with her world of documentary filmmaking.

After the era of my parents' fairy tales and bedtime stories, there came a time where we watched movies before bed. Some of my favorite stories were in the form of documentaries. David Attenborough's voice was the soundtrack of my childhood. Everything he told and showed in his documentary series expanded my imagination and love for nature. Later, when I saw documentaries like *Racing Extinction* and *An Inconvenient Truth*, it ignited a fire within me that never quite left. *Kiss the Ground*, Seaspiracy, *Pulau Plastik*...continued to grow that flame.

Sitting next to Flore in the car, I listened eagerly and nodded along as she told me about her son Sam and her daughter Rose. Looking out the window watching Bali passing by, I wondered what it would be like to grow up in a big city like Paris. At the same time, I knew I would not be Melati without Bali.

Flore said that Sam and Rose were so inspired by what we did with Bye Bye Plastic Bags. I smiled, thinking it would be nice to meet them. I turned to Flore and told her that we were not the only ones making a difference. There were many more of us young people everywhere around the world doing incredible things.

"We are everywhere!" I said, adding, "And not just working on issues of plastic pollution, but on so many issues!" I started to get excited. "I wish someone could tell our story from our perspective."

Like with all film crews, there comes a time where you have to say goodbye. When the moment came with Flore, it didn't feel like a goodbye at all. Saying goodbye to Flore felt like the beginning of something. We just didn't know it yet.

Soon after the ARTE documentary on Bye Bye Plastic Bags was released, Flore reached out again. She had really listened those years before, and now she had an idea! She wanted to tell the bigger story: one where it wasn't just about one or two girls in Bali, but about our generation and what we believe in. No wonder I jumped with excitement when Flore came back to me. She had heard me. She really had.

The moment I threw my graduation cap off, I signed this 17-page contract and entrusted my life for the next year (and more) to Flore and the production of the film *Bigger Than Us*. The film changed my life.

Wow, did we learn a lot. Once again, I found myself in a position like 12-year-old Melati starting Bye Bye Plastic Bags, with absolutely no idea what I was getting myself into, but excited nonetheless.

- The vision was there.
- The team was there.
- The capital was raised.
- The excitement was high.
- We were driven by something *bigger than us* (literally)

And most importantly: the story was there.

It was an adventure of a lifetime. I met amazing people that were doing things beyond anything I would ever be able to do. And there were a lot of heavier topics than I was exposed to every day. Stories and realities I had never even imagined before; stories and realities I was innocently protected from. Child marriages and fighting for your life to finish school, risking your life with every article you write.

It was very hard for me to plug myself in and out, in a way where I feel like I could continue being who I am without feeling bad about it. But, it's a story that needs to be told and heard. We were understanding that there is something a lot bigger than us.

Mohamad Al Jounde, Syria and Lebanon

When he was 12 years old, Mo had to flee his home country of Syria. The hardships and lessons he had to learn at his young age built a foundation for his work in education. He set up a school with other refugee kids in the camps in Lebanon, with the belief that school is a safe haven for children.

Mary Finn, Lesvos, Greece

Mary is a total badass. She is at the front lines saving lives, working with different organizations as a captain on refugee rescue boats. Mary has spent the last few years patrolling the waters between Turkey and Greece.

Winnie Tushabe, Uganda

I met Winnie when she was 8 months pregnant. She had garden boots on and shovels in her hand and asked if I wanted to go and see the gardens. Winnie works with the refugees in Uganda to build gardens.

Rene Silva, Río De Janeiro, Brazil

At 12 years old, Rene had enough of the way the media from the "outside" was talking about his country's favelas (impoverished neighborhoods). He felt they weren't portraying his community in an authentic way, so he started his own newspaper company to help fix the narrative from the inside.

Xiuhtezcatl Martinez, Colorado, USA

Xiuhtezcatl has been doing this work the longest. He is an artist who turns words into the most powerful tool for change. Through his music, he brings messages of indigenous wisdom and change all around the world.

Memory Banda, Malawi

Memory changed the legal marriage age for Malawi from 15 to 18 – all before she herself was 18! An incredible human full of energy and vision.

CHANGEMAKERS. GLOBALIZATION. FLOW.

Bigger Than Us was a vision that turned into reality because the story was there. We could hear it, see it, smell it – everything about it was so clear in our minds. We just did what we do best and told the story. Find the story, and the rest will follow.

LESSON #58: TRANSLATING STORIES INTO INCOME

Over the years, I have developed my skills of storytelling, and today, I have turned public speaking into my full-time career. It's still a funny thing to say every time someone asks, "What do you do?" *I'm a public speaker; I tell stories for a living.*

I have been really lucky to have had the support and network to turn this 12-year-old's dream into a full-time, self-sustaining career by age 19. I wouldn't have been able to do this without the incredible support system from the early days made up of individuals and organisations that believed in me.

People often looked confused when I told them, "I tell stories," so I used to try to move the conversation on quickly with, "What about you?" But soon after, they'd always ask a follow up question: "Wait, so you get paid to speak?"

The answer is *yes*. Not always, but I have been extremely privileged to work towards a platform where I do get paid for most of my speeches now. All speeches at schools are done for free or on a donation basis back to the organization. But nearly all of my corporate speaking engagements are paid for.

When I first started getting paid to speak, it felt weird. I definitely wasn't used to it, not that I am now either. It sometimes still feels like a strange exchange. However, I stand for the fact that the work that us changemakers bring into these spaces *should* be recognized financially as well. It is important, and it has value. Oftentimes, we have a perspective and a reality that is excluded from programs – which is all the more reason for us to be there. For many of us, taking the time away from our projects is an expensive exercise, so it is only fair that the time and energy is properly compensated just like any other CEO or "job" in the corporate world.

Turning your stories into income can look really different depending on platform, format, and duration. It really depends but it starts with the first invitation. How do we share these invitations to actually turn your stories into income? Well, it brings me to my next lesson:

LESSON #59: SHARING OPPORTUNITIES WITH OTHERS SPARKS JOY

When public speaking became my job and not a story I simply loved sharing, I found myself evolving to the next round of my life as a young changemaker. I had surpassed being that 16-year-old diplomat onstage. At 19 years old, I felt like a broken record player. They always asked the same questions. I always delivered the same stories. It became a performance, and I didn't know anymore how to find the spark.

The one thing that keeps me grounded at all of these different events and stages is the people I get to meet. The other young changemakers I get to hang out with. The backstage conversations and laughs we would have throughout the event.

Besides, being paid for your speaking engagements is actually one of the ways that allow us to be "full time" on our projects that often do not have any financial compensation. This funding model was something I wanted to make more accessible for other young changemakers globally. I realized that many of my friends, or even the changemakers we were working with at YOUTHTOPIA, didn't have the same support as I did when it came to securing financial compensation for their speaking engagements.

I wanted to extend the opportunity for more young changemakers to be professionally represented. While it is important for us to speak at these events and get compensated, what is even more important is that we are not censored or asked to change our stories. So, to make this vision of a speaking agency for young changemakers a reality, we needed an untraditional, willing, and leading bureau to say YES.

After years of receiving support from the London Speaker Bureau on an individual basis, I decided to share the big vision with them.

Today, in collaboration with the London Speaker Bureau, we are proud to share that we have built a speaking agency for young changemakers. It is a perfect partnership. YOUTHTOPIA has a network of incredible young changemakers, and the London Speaker Bureau has the network of conferences looking for these changemakers. And even better, LSB has the knowledge, experience, and all the willingness to represent our YOUTHTOPIA changemakers to ensure that we are fairly compensated at these events. All of this allows us changemakers to stick to what we do best: deliver the story of change.

Our speaking agency profiles young changemakers who are part of the YOUTHTOPIA Circle of Youth. In order to be part of this, you need to be:

- Between the ages of 12 and 25
- Have a track record of change
- Have your own project that covers a Sustainable Development Goal
- Have experience in public speaking (not necessarily paid public speaking yet)

Essentially, this partnership is foundational proof that young people are slowly entering these places as serious stakeholders and not just as inspiration.

BUT, there is still a lot of work to do…

LESSON #60: INSPIRATION IS WHERE CHANGE BEGINS

Inspiration used to annoy me, but here is what I learned

Sharing this opportunity with others helped me stay motivated, but there was still this feeling that I couldn't quite shake. At these conferences, people would always tell me, "You are so inspiring!" And it used to annoy me so much.

After a big stage, I would get physically sick because of how many people would come up to me, shake my hand, pass me their card, and squeeze my shoulders, all while saying, "You did great; you were inspiring up there." Didn't they understand it wasn't about being inspirational? We wanted action. We wanted change.

At the same time, I can't deny the adrenaline rush I feel after coming off a stage. It's always electric, and I can't wait to go into the crowd for some networking. I'm always a little nervous for that part, as it's not an experience catered to my strength. I feel like it's almost a social experiment: who comes up to you, what they say, how they say it, and interestingly, who does *not* come up to you and purposefully stays away. It shows you a lot about the comfort of people when it comes to change.

I once did a speech for an internal meeting with corporate leaders from all industries. It was a 45-minute Masterclass on sustainability and expectations of Gen Z. It was a slightly different format than I was used to, and the audience was tough, but I really enjoyed the long, interactive format. Afterwards, when I closed and the lecture hall doors opened once more, I realized that the only people coming up to me afterwards were women. And they all came at me with a motherly approach, not necessarily as someone to be taken seriously. "Oh you were so good." "So inspiring!" "Really top-notch!"

There was another time, where the audience of 1,500 business leaders erupted in applause as I closed my speech. I crumpled up the piece of paper that I brought with me onstage and did a little bow before walking off. The stairs towards backstage were dark, and I had to squint my eyes to make sure I could see everything clearly and didn't fall.

I made it backstage, and the adrenaline was pumping to my head as they took off my microphone. My "assistant" for the day then led me to the networking session. From backstage, we walked through long corridors with terrible lighting and pushed through some doors until we finally make it out into a big room. The sound in the room was loud. Everyone was busy talking to one another.

One by one, more and more people came up to me, shaking my hand in congratulations and telling me:

"You are such a confident speaker!"

"It was so inspiring to listen to you!"

"Such an inspiring session."

And with each comment, I grew more and more agitated. I was frustrated that they only felt *inspired*. I shared this with a mentor of mine one day, and they said, "Try to remember that inspiration is still the first step that people need to experience before they can implement any sort of action."

It all clicked then. I've seen the process for young changemakers to create change in our global community and I know they started from a place of being inspired too. Change is a journey that begins with:

Inspiration:
Where one feels inspired by others' actions and stories.
Then,

Education:
Where one feels called to learn more about the topics they were inspired about.

And then,

Implementation:
Where one takes ownership into implementing this knowledge into their own lives.

The demand for inspiration is high. We also see that with the speaking agency: there is no shortage of need when it comes to inspiration. It is the steps after that need a lot more attention: education and implementation. This is a reality that weighs heavily on our young shoulders. As we grow up, we begin to wonder where and when we let inspiration become a limitation instead of a beginning.

CHAPTER SIX:

GROWING UP & GENERATIONAL DIFFERENCES

Lessons in this chapter:

#61: This is not a sacrifice
#62: Activism is not defined by age
#63: Changemaking is a lifestyle
#64: Be present. Be your age. It's okay.
#65: Experiences shape our own truths
#66: The world is changing

A poem written in 2014
I was 13 years old

"Growing Up"

The girls in my class
grow up so fast
no Barbies but bras
no candies but boys
I'm not ready yet
I don't want to board the teenage jet
flying into the sky, with a new mind
leaving Winnie the Pooh and the princesses behind
I'm afraid of the land I will arrive on
shaky ground, nothing left, everything's gone
I'm stuck with the baby face
while the rest walk in miniskirts with such grace
the girls in my class say
"Grow up!"
But then who knows what the meaning of grow up means?
Does it mean to be wise and free or does it mean to be wearing
push-up bras and too much makeup?
So then I said
"No thanks, I'll stick to the candies and Barbies, Winnie the Pooh
and the princesses for just a bit longer,
I'm sure the jet can wait"
Turned on my heels and saw their faces filled with confusion
and I thought to myself
"Ha, the girls in my class grew up too fast"

THE DIFFERENT GENERATIONS

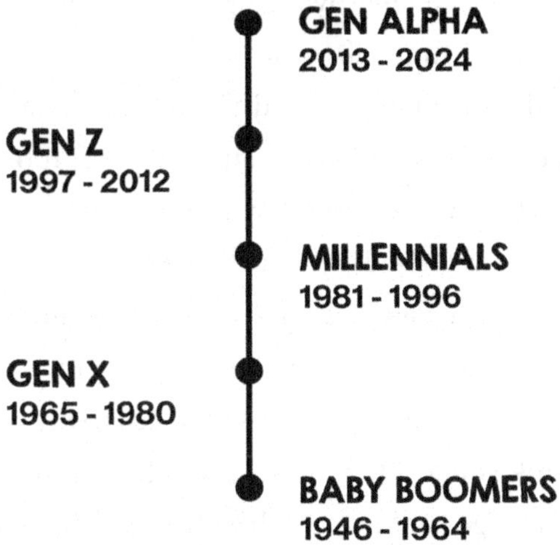

LESSON #61: THIS IS NOT A SACRIFICE

As changemakers, I feel like we're always talking about change. Change in this part of the world, or change in this department… but what about the changes *we* go through?

We're so young when we start, and growing up in this space exposes us to so much.

I've always been terrified of growing up. I'm not sure where it comes from exactly, but it's there: undeniable on every birthday and big moment that passes. Maybe it's because of many grown-ups' ignorance towards nature's destruction. Maybe it's because

I see how hard people work, with little to no purpose to that work.

Whenever I think about growing up, I get this terribly heavy feeling in my chest. If I think about it too long, I still get that feeling sometimes, as if I was eight years old all over again, frantically wanting to go home. There is actually a name for this fear of growing up: "adulting anxiety" or "Peter Pan syndrome." It's a psychological phenomenon characterized by reluctance towards the process of taking on adult responsibilities. This fear can manifest in various ways and can look a little different for each person. I don't think I have adulting anxiety, per se, but when I talked to my mum about it, she said: "I think you just had way too much adult responsibility at far too young an age, and now it's backfiring." That did put things into perspective a bit for me, because prior to that, I could never quite place it. At the same time, I do often get this question:

"Do you feel like you had to sacrifice your childhood?"

My answer is always no. I used to be quick to answer, with a rushed, "No," now that I think back to it. I wonder if I was just quick to answer because I wanted to defend the work I had been doing, like a loyal servant to the duty of changemaking. In hindsight, I realize that it was a lot of responsibility and weight on my shoulders. But there is a difference between a sacrifice and a responsibility.

I love what I do, and I never see my longer-than-a-decade career and contribution to the movement as a sacrifice of my childhood.

It wasn't one or the other for me. It never felt like I was missing out on anything, because it *was* my everything. I put all that I had into building the movement. My changemaking defined my childhood ... I never thought it was the other way around: that my youthful age defined my activism. But it was a narrative the world around me had decided, the story of a bunch of kids standing up for their island home went the most viral. This reality set an insanely high bar for my adulthood.

LESSON #62: ACTIVISM IS NOT DEFINED BY AGE

So, looking back at the Peter Pan syndrome and its many different influences, I do feel some relatable elements. Generally, here are some reasons why people experience Peter Pan syndrome:

- **Loss of Freedom:** Growing up often comes with increased responsibilities and expectations. For me, I felt it the most at graduation. I perceived that experience as a big moment where I knew life would never be the same, and my carefree aspect of childhood was slowly becoming a distant memory.
- **Fear of Failure:** Adulthood often involves taking on new roles and responsibilities, and the fear of failure in these areas can be a significant source of anxiety. The pressure to succeed in various aspects of life may contribute to a fear of not measuring up.
- **Loss of Childhood Innocence:** Personally, I've always been serious, and maybe that's why this factor of loss of childhood inno-

cence is so strange to me. The older I became, the more I wanted life to be *simple.* I craved that childhood innocence and simplicity, and I realized I may have taken it for granted.

- **Attachment to the Past:** Some people may have a deep emotional attachment to their past. I know I do. Childhood memories and relationships are all so nostalgic to think back on. The fear of growing up can be rooted in a reluctance to let go of these cherished aspects of life. My childhood was filled with insane opportunities, and I've developed so many memories and beautiful moments that I don't want to let go of.

Or maybe I'm afraid of getting older because my entire "career" is attached to my age: "12-year-old Melati; 17 year-old changemaker."

Turning 18 is supposed to be something you're excited about. But unlike most excited-for-independence teenagers, my 18th birthday was what I feared the most. Not many people understood why. Actually, almost everybody thought it was strange. I didn't know if I really understood why I was so scared, and I most definitely thought it was strange. All I remember is that, leading up towards the day of my 18th birthday, I strongly wished that I could give my birthday back. I didn't want to turn 18. I wanted to turn back time because all of my life, and now my "career," revolved around a specific introduction:

"Hi, my name is Melati, and I'm 12."

Stranger number one: "Oh my goodness! You're 12 years old?!"

"Hi, my name is Melati, I'm 13."

Stranger number two: "Oh my goodness! What did I do when I was 13 years old?!"

"I'm 14, 15, 16, 17..."

Saying "I'm 18 years old," just seemed too old – like suddenly (or *finally*, for most of my peers), I was seen as a young adult. No more youthful or childish behavior. It scared me and made me feel like I was about to lose one of the biggest parts of my identity as a changemaker: my youthful age.

There is something to say here about how we romanticize the youth movement, particularly youth activists who have a certain amount of spotlight on them. The headlines don't become headlines without the age attached.

On the morning of my 18th birthday, I woke up surrounded by family and friends. I could finally see that just because I turned 18 didn't mean that I would stop being a changemaker. Young, old, excited, frustrated, sad, happy: this is the work I will do forever.

TEENAGER. AGE. TIME.

LESSON #63: CHANGEMAKING IS A LIFESTYLE

Changemaking is something you do every day. It starts the minute you wake up and is carried by your actions and decisions throughout the day until you go to sleep. While they can be big or small actions, one thing became clear to me: changemaking is a lifestyle.

FOREVER. LIFELONG. REALIZATION.

But still, this feeling of closing chapters came again a couple months earlier, when it was time to graduate high school.

What was I thinking when I graduated?

On a June afternoon in Bali, our class began changing into our graduation robes. It became even hotter and stickier underneath the thick material of the long garment. Slowly, one by one, we walked down to the main ceremony hall. The entire path was decorated with flowers, and our whole school sat waiting on the open field. It was stunning. Beautiful, natural decorations covered each corner. Our class sat in a row at the front of the crowd.

I looked back, and I could see my family and my two best friends that flew over especially for the occasion. I smiled, and my heart squeezed a little bit. This was it. This was the end of my high school education. After this, what was next?

I think I'm going to faint. I looked around desperately for some water, and a fan to try to cool down, but before I could get up, the MC started the program.

"Today, we have gathered around to celebrate our grade 12 students…"

Okay, here we go.

As they called out our names, I watched as my friends went up to collect their diplomas. Each time a student went up, the crowd exploded in loud cheers. For every student, the same amount of enthusiasm. I cried every single time.

But when it was my turn, the tears turned from happy to … sad? anxious? fearful? I'm not really sure what it was exactly. When they called my name to receive my high school diploma, I wanted to run in the opposite direction. I wanted to stay a "forever student." It's kind of funny to think back on it now, but I was genuinely worried about several things:

- Up until now, all my excuses for late email responses had been: "Sorry for not replying sooner, school has been so busy!" What would I say now?
- When attending an event seemed like too much, I would say: "I won't be able to make it to the conference because I have school." What reason did I have now?
- And how would I even structure my day without school?

School was a part of my life that I must honestly say came to an end too soon. I wanted it to last longer.

But I decided to change my narrative and focus on the positives: I was gonna GRAB that diploma. I worked hard to leave school a year early.

When I was in this mindset, instead of worrying, I was thinking about the positives:

- I finally can spend time in my inbox and properly connect with people.
- I finally can go to all those conferences and events.
- I finally can fill my days with meaningful connections and work on things that matter to me and the movement.

Suddenly, I had graduated high school a year early, I had turned 18 and was filled with so much life and energy within me. My new opening became:

"Hi, my name is Melati. I'm 18 years old and a full-time changemaker."

So, changemaking really is a lifestyle that we can all choose. Being a changemaker simply means a person who wakes up and thinks, "How can I make the world around me a little bit better today?" If we think about it like that, many of the decisions we make every day can act as a small gesture of changemaking. What will you eat today? What brands will you support? How will you move around the city? Who will you vote for?

Changemaking as a lifestyle means that we become intentional with our actions and decisions. You don't have to wait to practice daily changemaking until you work at a specific organization. Changemaking doesn't really fit the 9-to-5 anyway.

I realized I had been doing this long before I graduated and was ready to continue to make it my full-time focus.

ANTICIPATION. TRANSITION. IDENTITY.

LESSON #64: BE PRESENT. BE YOUR AGE. I TS OKAY.

I never used to understand it when people would say, "You should also have time to be a 16-year-old, Melati." Or sometimes I'd hear, "Do you ever do things that a normal 16-year-old does?"

Immediately, I would think, "Time to be 16 years old? You think we have time?!!!!" Our planet is literally dying. We are running *out* of time and, besides, why can't adults make time to be responsible leaders then? I would also think to myself, "What does a normal 16-year-old even do nowadays?"

Recognizing where we are in life, at whatever age, allows us to build self-awareness and learn so much about ourselves. As we grow older, we change. Our views on life, our goals, our friends. We are constantly changing, and creating space to be present and aware of those changes only builds a strong foundation for ourselves.

However, it's also important to recognize that times change too. The reality of our childhoods and our parents' childhoods are incomparable. As a 16-year-old, I couldn't imagine doing anything else with my time because of the world we live in. But for my parents' generation, 16 years old was probably supposed to mean school, your first love, good grades, prom, and that's about it.

PRESENCE. LIFE. EVOLUTION.

LESSON #65: EXPERIENCES SHAPE OUR OWN TRUTHS

There is a theory as to why generations have a hard time understanding one another. It's called the "Shifting Baseline Syndrome." It is when our own reality, shaped by experiences and cultural relevance related to our time, does not translate over to the next, new, or old generation, because of the realities they experienced. Over time, changes across generations often become accepted as the status quo or "the way things have always been." Essentially, it is a gradual change in our accepted norms and expectations, until the next generation comes along with their new norms and expectations creating that *shift*.

Understanding this simple lesson will take a lot of frustration out of creating change across generations. Let's take a simple example of making a phone call. People who grew up in the '60s remember the telephone experience as dialing the numbers in by spinning this wheel to each number. It was a slow process that required patience and actually knowing the number that you wanted to call.

Fast forward a bit, and there was a whole era where flip phones were the coolest thing on Earth. You could choose your unique ringtone and put stickers on your phone. Three clicks on the same button to get to the letter C for a text, and then two clicks for H, and you eventually spelled out the word CHANGE. This was a whole different level of patience, but it was cool. I remember that era slightly from when I was a little kid and would look at all the teenagers and their cool phones, dazzling with stickers. I thought, "One day, I'll have my own..."

But now, look at my generation and how we experience the telephone. First of all, we don't even call it a telephone anymore. It's a *phone*. Even more precisely, an iPhone: as if it has become a part of me, myself, and I. Our generation very rarely calls. We text. We DM. We tweet. None of us memorize a number unless it's our parents' for an emergency. And if we do call, it's: "Hey Siri, call Nicholas."

My mum still writes important phone numbers in a book. She would never use "hey Siri" to call someone. She has very little understanding as to why we use our phones the way we do, because for her childhood, a phone was just for calling. Again, another stark baseline shift that prevents generations from understanding one another. For us Gen Zers, it's impossible to think a phone is just for calling. I personally use my phone for work emails, private chats with friends, my professional calendar and scheduling, booking my holidays, finding interesting research, and uploading my life updates through social media. And that's just to name a few of the things my phone enables me to do.

So, baseline shift: it's very real and very present.

What about another example of the baseline shift, but when it comes to sustainability? I think that word in itself is a baseline shift. It seems strange to imagine, but the "sustainability" concept as we know it today dates back to less than 30 years ago. I met the woman who spearheaded a commission that produced this report for the UN.

The famous Brundtland Report, also entitled "Our Common Future," was asked to create "A global agenda for change" - or at least in her opening statement, Gro Brundtland shares "this was what the World Commission on Environment and Development was asked to formulate. It was an urgent call by the General Assembly of the United Nations to:

- Propose long-term environmental strategies for achieving sustainable development by the year 2000 and beyond
- Recommend ways that concern for the environment may be translated into greater cooperation among developing countries and between countries at different stages of economic and social development, and lead to the achievement of common and mutually supportive objectives that take account of the interrelationships between people, resources, environment, and development
- Consider ways and means by which the international community can deal more effectively with environment concerns
- Help define shared perceptions of long-term environmental issues and the appropriate efforts needed to deal successfully with the problems of protecting and enhancing the environment, a long-term agenda for action during the coming decades, as well as aspirational goals for the world community

The Brundtland Report created a foundation for the modern world to understand what sustainability was, and how to move forward within the planetary boundaries.

But, even before this report, sustainability always existed, albeit it in simple ways. For example, my mum could point to aspects of her life growing up in the Netherlands that were sustainable, like the milkman. Each week, a man on a bicycle with a cart filled with glass bottles with milk would stop by to make a delivery. As the youngest in her family, it was my mum's job to make sure the bottles were washed after use and returned to the community center. This was a circular loop in its simplest form. It didn't get more sustainable than that at the time.

And look at Tri Hita Karana, explained in the first chapter as the traditional way of life for the Balinese that has existed for centuries. A sustainable lifestyle in harmony with three elements: the natural world, the community, and your own self-awareness. Sustainability in its truest form.

However, our generations are very different, baseline shift or not. I think that's what always makes a time in history unique: the differences between generations, and how we are able to challenge and complement each other to move our societies forward.

Over the last 70 years, people have never lived so well. We live longer lives, are better fed, are more educated, and travel a lot more. But where is the line between degrading the nature in return for the lifestyle?

Let's look at five different aspects in life and how we view, interact, and move forward with all of them. The examples I chose showcase, at a macro level, how differently our generations view things due to the shifting baseline syndrome.

1) Destruction of Nature
2) Economics
3) The Trust Economy
4) The World of Work
5) Education & the Way We Learn

LESSON #66: THE WORLD IS CHANGING

Destruction of nature

Gen Zer Sage Lenier is a climate activist in New York City. One day, onstage, she was asked by a journalist about how she felt about the radical actions of activists. This was what she was asked: "Over the course of the last few months, we have seen an escalation of these protests. We're talking about slashing tires, breaking windows, and even throwing paint at some ministers. The question to you is: do you support what some consider a more radical take?"

Her answer was spot-on. She calmly nodded her head as the question was asked, smiled, and when it was her turn to answer, she spoke a powerful truth. She started off by saying that we first needed to have a conversation about what constitutes violence. "Why is it okay for business leaders and politicians to displace indigenous people and raze entire forests in order to drill oil or harvest lumber, and that's not considered violence, but slashing tires is? It's actually a very minor inconvenience for them [the ministers] – they have five cars – so I don't really want to fully answer the question because I do think we need a very radical approach to a very, very dire problem." She continued to explain that as a collective, we were beginning to understand how inconveniencing politicians and business leaders could let them know that we were not just going to lie down and die the way we are on track for. Three degrees of warming by 2100 means mass suffering, and it could potentially mean the loss of hundreds of millions of lives. "So I would like for those business leaders to be asked questions about the violence they raise," she said.

Talking about business leaders, let's see another generation's perspective on this topic of the destruction of nature. Former CEO of Whole Foods and member of the baby boomer generation, John Mackey, publicly said that there "no scientific consensus exists" regarding the cause of climate change. He confidently added that it would be a pity to allow "hysteria about global warming" to cause us "to raise taxes and increase regulation, and in turn, lower our standard of living and lead to an increase in poverty."

This shows how differently two generations can view the destruction of nature. With each generation, we see a majority shift in what we decide to value, based on our own experiences and lived reality.

"An oil spill in the sea can be considered a casualty of a business move for one generation, and a complete catastrophe for another generation.
For one generation, the expansion of more fossil fuel rigs is considered a profitable investment; for another, it means signing our own death certificate.
is a dead tree more valuable than a living tree? Are wild and alive fish less valuable than fine dining sushi?"

Economics

As the industrial & linear economy was booming, there was a light at the end of the tunnel as Sir Partha Dasgupta tried to connect our economy and its relationship to nature. His father, the noted economist Amiya Kumar Dasgupta, had a huge influence on him and his path towards academia. After completing a bachelor's degree in physics in Delhi, Dasgupta moved to the United Kingdom, where he studied mathematics and later gained a doctorate in economics.

So what's the connection between our economy and nature? Dasgupta's Economics of Biodiversity paper warned that critical ecosystems, from coral reefs to rainforests, are nearing dangerous tipping points, with catastrophic consequences for economies and people's well-being.

The 600-page report called for a fundamental rethink of humanity's relationship with nature and how it is valued, arguing that the failure to include "ecosystem services" on national balance sheets has only intensified the exploitation of the natural world.

"[It is] about introducing nature as a capital asset into economic thinking and showing how economic possibilities are entirely dependent on this finite entity," said Dasgupta.

In one of the videos he produced with the United Nations Environment Program, he explained that traditionally, when you read an economic forecast, it shows investment in factories, employment rates, or GDP growth.

"They never mention what's happening to the ecosystems. So I really tried to reconstruct economics by placing the human economy as embedded in nature."

Dasgupta's work focuses on the productivity of nature, showing how economic possibilities are entirely dependent on this finite entity we call nature. He continued to say, "Global demand for nature's goods and services exceeds nature's ability to supply them on a sustainable basis. Mother Nature can be depreciated like that. You simply cut the forest. It's gone."

He added, "When you pump carbon dioxide into the atmosphere, that's like depreciating the atmosphere. Now, GDP will not count that destruction. You could have a growing economy, but they've put a huge pressure on the biosphere, leading to biodiversity loss, climate change. So, I think the way we measure economic success or failure needs to be built with this in mind."

Not all is lost as boomers like Dasgupta work in line with some of our shared values, but we know that even this concept of nature & economy has not taken full potential implementation in the modern world of today. In addition to the connection that the economy has with nature, there is another interesting development happening that has nothing to do with actual "capital." It is something that has grown bigger and bigger over the last technological rise, affecting later generations. It's called the trust economy.

The trust economy

I say that this has nothing to do with actual "capital," but really, the *new* currency of the economy is trust. If people do not trust your product, your story, your reputation, then they will turn away, join another group, or buy from a different company.

Collaborative consumption marketplaces empower platforms like Airbnb or Uber to use technology to build trust between strangers. Amongst community feedback and ratings, a new trust economy begins to grow. The development of technologies has enabled us to match wants with haves in more democratic and faster ways than ever before. Not only is this changing the way we see traditional "economical" structures, i.e., the way supply and demand works, but it is also the start of a massive value shift. The trust economy puts a focus on reputation, transparency, authenticity, and reliability – all based on consumer experience and feedback.

It's literally placing the power back into the hands of the consumer.

I bring this up because it is vital to understand the trust economy in order to mobilize change to happen. As technology and digital platforms have expanded, trust has become essential for growth. With so much going on, we essentially have created an oversaturated, overload of information. Because of this, we now live in a broken trust system. Things like greenwashing or big, empty political promises have widened the gap of mistrust between generations even more.

There is a disconnect between companies, leaders, and consumers; a good, everyday example of this is the rapid change in the world of work.

The world of work

The question of, "What do you want to be when you grow up" asked of young people is now a tricky one, because most of the jobs kids will *say* they want to be will no longer exist by the time they enter the workforce.

"85% of the jobs that will exist in 2030 haven't even been invented yet," according to a report published by Dell Technologies and authored by the Institute for the Future (IFTF) and a panel of 20 tech, business, and academic experts from around the world.

Changemaking, however, often isn't even seen as a "real job." It still falls into the "passion project" category and as seen as a hobby, an after-school project, or a phase.

This is another big generational difference. The world of work is changing so much and so rapidly. The pandemic forced millions of us, both as individuals and companies, to change the way we work. Offices shut down, our living rooms became multidimensional Zoom rooms and family spaces.

So, preparing for a job that doesn't exist yet creates a challenging path to navigate. Imagine those who go into a four-year study program, only to enter the workforce with outdated knowledge. How does this lesson allow us to prepare and perhaps change the way we look at learning?

"You can't teach about things that don't exist yet, but you can teach someone to learn how to learn." – Leo Salemi

Education & the way we learn

I was so lucky to be a scholarship student at the Green School Bali, a school built from bamboo with the philosophy that nature is our biggest teacher. The founders of the school, John and

Cynthia Hardy, paved the way for us to have the foundational support during our school years, balancing changemaking and classes. Without their support, alongside my teachers, I would be nowhere.

This bamboo cathedral of a school also shaped my views on the educational industry: it's an industry that needs a massive revolution. Our classrooms need to reflect the outside world and act as an incubator on how to improve what no longer works, from making it mandatory to teach climate science and communications to encouraging something as simple as normalizing gap years.

It's another very traditional, and yet still expected, path of life from Baby Boomers to Gen Z that we must go to university right after high school graduation. This is purely coming, again, from their lived realities of what the norm was when they were in high school.

For older generations, after high school, they either started working or went to college. Gap years did not become "a thing" until the 1960s, when the young, baby boom generation wanted to get away from the severity of their parent's generation (which was influenced by war). A baseline shift between generations: imagine what that was like.

At first, the primary purpose of the gap year was for countries to exchange cultural ideals in the hope of preventing future wars. Fast forward a bit into the future, and we see that a major boost to the concept of gap years was given when it got the royal stamp of approval in Britain with Prince William taking a gap year before starting at St. Andrew's University in Scotland. The gap year was given great attention again when President Obama's daughter Malia took a gap year after high school before attending Harvard.

I took a gap year. Actually, I took several gap years. Technically, I'm not sure if it still counts, but I think I'm still on my gap year. The point is, I didn't follow the traditional educational pathway that is set for us, which usually looks like this:

Pre-school > middle school > high school > college > life begins

My education journey looked a little something like this:

Pre-school > middle school > homeschool > 3-month travel around the world > high school > skip a grade > graduate a year early with all my required credits and more > gap year > filmed a documentary > built a company > still learning every day

It might be messy from a first glance, but I wouldn't do it any differently if I had the choice. Taking a gap year is a personal choice. I graduated early and took a gap year because:

- I had time and support.
- There was no pressure.
- My activism work was at its peak, and I didn't want to lose momentum by going away to a campus for four years.

In my gap year, I traveled the world, met other changemakers, filmed the documentary *Bigger Than Us*, which premiered at the Cannes Film Festival, started working on my new company full time, built an office … the list goes on.

But on a more personal note, I developed a strong sense of self-awareness. I went on a silent retreat. I volunteered at different community projects. I learned so much about myself in different situations. Most importantly, I felt like I gave myself time to explore the world and explore myself.

I highly recommend gap years solely just for that opportunity of exploration. But here there a few things to consider when you make the decision for a gap year or not.

Questions to ask yourself before taking a gap year

Determine why you're considering taking a gap year

- You want a break from academics?
- You don't know what school you want to go to next?
- You're unsure if you want to go to school at all?

Talk to your support system

- Are they supportive of the idea of a gap year?
- Do they think this is an option for you?
- Is this something feasible to do cost-wise, etc.?

Figure out what you want to do in your gap year, and make sure it benefits you:

- Personally
- Professionally
- Academically

And last but not least, give yourself an idea of how much time you want to take for your gap year. Like I said, for me personally, my gap year turned into gap *years*. But that was okay for me because I found my career and was focusing on the development of my activism. I wasn't pressured nor did I personally feel the pressure to go to university yet. But if that foundation is not so clear to you, consider giving yourself a time frame to check in and continue with your learning experience.

The university talk

One day, years after the decision of my gap year, I sat at an exclusive lunch with CEOs. We were in the big city, and they had rented out an entire part of the restaurant just for our lunch. It was over-the-top fancy for 1 p.m. on a random, unimportant Tuesday. I sat down next to one CEO of a multinational company, and we hit it off. Throughout the lunch, there were moments in my story that would cause the whole table to pause and listen.

"And then, after 48 hours of our food strike, we finally got the call from the governor's office…"

We talked a lot about youth-led change and how we've already achieved so much in our short years. And then the question came up. It always does.

"What about university? What would you like to study, Melati?"

Indeed, what would I like to study? The list is long. But I believe that I've already started this learning journey since I was 12 years old. Of course there is still so much to learn.

But I refuse to believe that the only way for things to be learned is in the four walls of a lecture hall. My "professors" are other entrepreneurs, politicians, scientists, and youth leaders. My classroom is the conference rooms, team meetings, networking galas, beach cleanups, and protests on the streets.

So, this is what I told the CEO sitting next to me. He put his fork down, wiped his mouth with his handkerchief, and turned his body to fully face me. *Here we go again,* I thought to myself as I braced for what was about to happen.

What happened next was a mini lecture on why it is important to go to school. "Not only for your academic excellence, but also for your social skills, Melati." The noise around me usually drowns out when this happens, and I feel myself biting my tongue. I watched his mouth move, his hand gestures decisive and stern. He was not telling me it was a good idea. He was telling me it was the only reasonable next step. He did not like that I did not go to university yet.

I simply nodded along as I listened to his side of the story and concluded by saying, "Well, the good news is that university won't go anywhere. When I am ready, it will be right there waiting for me."

Later, the organizer pulled me aside and said that she overheard the conversation about university. "It might be worth going to university because that's just what the corporate world expects," she added pointedly. This often made me upset in the past because I was frustrated how people still needed traditional validation to prove that you've "learned" something. A normal university bachelor program is between three and four years. I had been doing this work for over six years before I even reached the age to be able to go to university.

I strongly believe that changing the ways we value and recognize our learning experiences will help us move towards a more kind education system that empowers us all.

I walked a fine line in the luncheon situation that I was in. When it comes to partnerships and intergenerational connections, you don't want to upset and disappoint your new partners with your personal decision; and at the same time, you hope they don't hold it against you in a professional manner.

One time, I was heavily interrogated by a mentor who played devil's advocate. "Melati, how are you building an educational platform with YOUTHTOPIA, but you haven't even gone to university?"

DAMN. That one knocked me on my ass. It sure is one way to look at it, and there are many people who may look at it that way. I had no idea. It didn't even cross my mind! Do we really still measure success based on the linear education process? It felt like suddenly the 10 years of work I had led with Bye Bye Plastic Bags was thrown out the window. It wasn't enough proof of my commitment and my skill to build YOUTHTOPIA.

YOUTHTOPIA

Ironically, this is one of the reasons why I built YOUTHTOPIA: to help give more young people the platform and opportunities to be taken seriously. After a decade with Bye Bye Plastic Bags, my interests in the world of changemaking only started to grow. I was growing up myself, and I guess that naturally is what happens. Your interests expand. I was asking more questions than ever.

At 18 years old, I had already visited more than 30 countries, met with presidents and prime ministers, international celebrities, and local heroes. But the biggest group I had connected with were young people. I had already spoken to over 1 million students all over the world.

I spent more time in other students' classrooms than my own classroom. As you can imagine, my teachers and parents were not too happy about that. But the point is, I learned so much. Like I said, my professors were other changemakers and CEOs and scientists. But my peers were also my teachers, students from around the world with different opinions and backgrounds. Students with different ideas and challenges locally who shared questions and curiosities. The exchange always ignited a fire deep within me.

In these conversations, there was always one question that resurfaced over and over again. Different faces, different countries, but the question remained the same.

"How do we create change? Where do we start?"

It never felt like I had enough time to answer this question. So simple, and yet, the beginning of something life-changing. The school bell would ring or the next speaker would come onstage, signaling the end of my session. The room would pack up and shift, and life would continue, except for this lingering feeling of an unanswered question. It grew so big that it turned into a vision. I was impatient to share it with the world. Something I believed could be a new story for us all to believe in: YOUTHTOPIA.

Together, with hundreds of young changemakers around the world, we created a free learning platform where young people can learn from each other about how to create change. To date, we have hundreds of programs led by influential changemakers, both studio-produced and selfie-style vlog content on our learning platform that shares basic changemaker skills.

So, essentially, we built our own mini university.

This brings me back to that fancy lunch. I could have found it frustrating when that CEO ridiculed me for not following the traditional way; and in that moment, I did. But it also fed my curiosity. There was such a strong belief in how education and experience go hand in hand. You learn by doing, and you learn over time.

Instead of wasting time pointing fingers and blaming one another, like we so often do, why not change the way we look at things? Baby Boomers do have one thing that many of us Gen Zers do not have yet. They have *experience*. Oftentimes, many of us Gen Zers have yet to accumulate this in life. On the other hand, Gen Z have a lot of passion and a sharp focus for the future, which Baby Boomers often have lost along the way. Trust me, there's a lot to unpack here because the potential is HUGE, so I've dedicated the whole next chapter to it.

There are still days where I sit down and wonder if the youth movement is only so impressive because of our age. As I grow up, I learn that there is power in holding onto your childhood dreams, energy, and vision, but there is also power in stepping into who you are today. Take all the dreams, energy, visions and run with them.

I know now the strength our generation brings to the world.

> *We cannot solve the problems with the same thinking that created them, and that is why intergenerational collaboration is so needed. That is why growing up can also be SO exciting.*

Yes, my age was a foundational reason that made my story jump out. It *was* a headliner. But that isn't the whole story.

I am not 12 years old anymore. I am entering the adult world with everyone else. There is still a lot to learn, but I am letting go of the Peter Pan syndrome and understanding more about what makes our generation unique, as well as the challenges and the divide that those differences can create. Soon, my focus shifted to finding ways where we could work together. It seemed like combining the strengths of both generations was the key to accelerate solutions for our rapidly dying world.

CHAPTER SEVEN:

HOW TO WORK TOGETHER

Lessons in this chapter:

#67: Greenwashing is so over
#68: Youthwashing happens, and it sucks
#69: Give, Go, Offer (the go with 2 g's)
#70: Our differences CAN BE OUR strengths
#71: The power of mentors
#72-77: The do's & don'ts for finding a mentor
#78: How to establish a good collaboration

Young people today are getting involved in changemaking at a younger and younger age. In fact, it's gotten to a point where I feel I'm almost the oldest "youth" in the room. At the same time, we're see the complete opposite age group realizing their role and understanding that it is never too late to create change. So perhaps age really is just a number? And we all pay way too much attention to it.

However, there is something to be said about young people at the forefront of many social and environmental changes throughout history. There is something youthful and creative and refreshing to our way of leading change. And perhaps it does have to do with our courage in our younger years, the less "jaded" we are, the less "stuck" and "strict" we are about a certain way of life. We challenge the status quo.

Let's take a quick look at some examples where young people have been at the forefront of change throughout history.

Claudette Colvin (born 1939): Before Rosa Parks, Claudette Colvin, a 15-year-old African American girl, refused to give up her bus seat to a white woman in Montgomery, Alabama, in 1955. Her arrest preceded the Montgomery Bus Boycott and was a significant act of resistance against racial segregation.

Anne Frank (1929-1945): Anne Frank, a Jewish girl, documented her experience of hiding from the Nazis during World War II in her diary. Her writings, published posthumously, have become a powerful account of the Holocaust and an enduring symbol of the impact of war on young lives.

More recently, and a personal idol of mine, **Malala Yousafzai** (born 1997): Malala, a Pakistani activist for female education, was shot by the Taliban at the age of 15 for her advocacy. Despite the attempt on her life, Malala continued to speak out for the right to education, especially for girls. In 2014, she became the youngest-ever Nobel Prize laureate.

These three examples highlight how young individuals have long been changemakers, challenging societal norms, advocating for human rights, and influencing historical events. Their actions demonstrate that age is not a barrier to making a significant impact on the world.

Jumping back into this day and age, especially in the last few years of the early 2020s, we have seen the rise of youth like never before, thanks to tools like social media and other technologies.

5 incredible and young changemakers today

1) Greta Thunberg

A young Swedish girl who is most known for her work with Fridays for the Future: a movement that began with her striking outside of the parliament with a sign titled: "School Strike for Climate."

2) Sophia Kianni

An Iranian-American social entrepreneur and activist. She is the founder and executive director of Climate Cardinals, which focuses on the power of language and helps to translate scientific reports into many different languages. Sophia is also the youngest United Nations advisor in U.S. history.

3) Helena Gualinga

An Ecuadorian environmental and human rights activist from the Kichwa Sarayaku community in Ecuador. She co-founded the organization Polluters Out and now leads a global movement of youth that demands the removal of fossil fuels from Indigenous lands, world governments, and international policy.

4) Gab Mejía

Gab is a conservation photographer and environmental storyteller. He is a National Geographic Explorer covering stories on nature, wildlife, the climate crisis, and Indigenous people. He has published stories in National Geographic, CNN, Nikon, The Manila Times, WWF, UNDP, and other international organizations and media platforms. He is the co-founder and communications and outreach lead of Youth Engaged in Wetlands, the global youth network advocating for the conservation of wetlands and natural-climate solutions around the world.

5) Louise Mabulo

Louise is a chef, farmer, and entrepreneur. She is the founder of The Cacao Project, a social venture aimed at equipping farmers for sustainable success, ensuring food security, and establishing resilient livelihoods. Louise is a featured honoree of Forbes Asia Under 30 and is a Young Champion of the Earth under the United Nations Environment Program. She is a recipient of the Friend Of Humanity Award under Friendship Ambassadors Foundation New York, Social Entrepreneur award from the University of Connecticut, and Champion for Sustainability Award from the Economic Times India.

All of these changemakers started between the ages of 12 and 15 years old. Collectively, today, they have a network of about 5 million people. And I am lucky to call them my friends. For many of us, we've grown up together at many of the international conferences, spent so much of our childhoods brainstorming campaigns, and when we grew old enough, we turned the cities we traveled to into our biggest playgrounds; talking to ministers before lunch and then rushing off to an after-party or festival.

We are not always together and often go months before seeing each other again. But our generation is interconnected through technologies available to us every second of the day. In fact, 56% of Gen Z relies on social media for communication (Gitnux).

The global community suddenly becomes available through one click of a button. In all corners of the world, from the story of two little sisters in Bali to the girl with the sign on the steps outside parliament in Sweden to kids in Colorado rapping about the environment, students globally have begun to stand up for things they believe in.

Millions of youth are taking to the streets, mobilizing and organizing. Since 2018, when Greta held her first strike, there have been thousands of strikes all around the globe, where students show the world that they are taking a stand. It's inspiring to see this resilience and yet, there is a new scary trend emerging: *youthwashing.*

It happened to me and countless others, because it's easier to do than you think. Together, in this chapter, we'll learn some practical ways to navigate it and work towards more meaningful collaborations. Before we dive into the topic of *youthwashing,* however, let's take a look at something that is more familiar: *greenwashing.*

LESSON #67: GREENWASHING IS SO OVER

It's a wild guess, but those of you who are reading this book hopefully (fingers crossed) know the term *greenwashing.*

Environmentalist Jay Westerveld coined the term "greenwashing" in 1986, in a critical essay inspired by the irony of the "save the towel" movement in hotels that had little impact beyond saving hotels money in laundry costs.

Greenwashing Definition

> *The act or practice of making a product, policy, activity, etc. appear to be more environmentally friendly or less environmentally damaging than it really is.*

The days of greenwashing are coming to an end, but it still happens in broad daylight. Let's look at an article published by Eco Experts on some of the worst examples that contributed to greenwashing.

From an article written by Josh Jackman, he highlights a list of 11 of the worst examples of greenwashing in 2023 globally. In summary, industries in the financial or sporting world have been most frequently found guilty of greenwashing. For example, banks or world sport tournaments have been caught sharing a message of a "sustainable promise", only for their actions to not measure up, by either failing miserably with the investments they promised or failing to reach climate goals they set.

Industries that support product platforms for online shopping and airlines have also been found guilty of greenwashing. In their messaging, they published commitments of less plastic, fewer emissions, and, yet, the final result varies and often does not add up to the promise.

What we see is that companies are often the ones accelerating the damages to our planet, with greenwashing and their actions.

In fact, 70% of emissions are by 100 companies alone.

Companies are being taken to court, but so are countries (more on this in the later chapters). Luckily, the tolerance for greenwashing is at an all-time low. It simply won't work anymore, not with Gen Z.

Greenwashing isn't the only "trend" that developed over the years. Activism has seen many different waves of "washings":

WHITE WASHING: The attempt to stop people from finding out the true facts about a situation. For example, brands that do not take responsibility when tragedies like the Rana Plaza collapse happen, yet are at the core of the issue.

BROWN WASHING: Trying to appear supportive of Black, Brown, Indigenous, and People of Color while not implementing anti-racist and/or BIPOC-empowering circumstances into their own business.

PINK WASHING: The promotion of female empowerment through advertisements, product messaging, or further brand communication while hiding one's own exploitative and/or unequal practices towards women.

RAINBOW WASHING: Trying to appear as being supportive of LGBTQIIA+ movement while not empowering LGBTQIIA+ individuals inside of their own business.

LESSON #68: YOUTHWASHING HAPPENS, AND IT SUCKS

So, youthwashing: what is it?

Youthwashing refers to young people's voices being used in a performative way, without paying attention to them or acting on concerns raised by this group in the long term. Put simply: young people are the new trend used for a very surface-level engagement with corporations. The intention also stays very limited to promotional material only, like a stage or anything front-facing to the public and not reflected internally.

So we can only ask the question:

Are we being taken seriously?

Or are we stuck at being only inspirational?

As a young changemaker myself, I've struggled with this on an ongoing basis. My first encounter with youthwashing was at 13 years old. I skipped school to attend a government meeting in Denpasar, our capital city, early in the morning. We woke up before the sunrise to drive from our home in the south of the island into the hustle and bustle of the city center. When I entered the room, a government official said to me, "Are you sure you want to do this type of work? You're so beautiful you could be a model."

Youthwashing, yes, but also all types of wrong. Putting me down as just a girl without any rights to be in that room, assuming I'm all beauty and no brains.

I noticed that our age and our gender stood out to people more and more. For example, when we released our TED Talk, the number one comment that would pop up over and over again would be something along the lines of:

"Oh it's amazing that you're so young and even more impressive that they are both young *girls*!"

What's interesting to me is that personally for my sister and I, we were raised to never allow those two things to hold us back. We looked at them as superpowers, assets to what makes us special, nothing less and nothing more.

Why does YOUTHWASHING happen?

This is a great question. I think it's a mix of many things: not knowing any better, not the right pairings, not enough capacity. The generational differences we explored in the previous chapter also play a factor to why youthwashing can take place.

But there are also reasons from Gen Z, like our hesitation to work with the private or public sector and more traditional settings. There is a large amount of distrust, the lack of belief that anything we say or do will be implemented to change anything. So this divide keeps us from understanding one another.

We also can take a look at the report by the We Are Family Foundation. This groundbreaking global study, Collaborating Across Generations: Insights, Challenges, and Best Practices, was conducted in late 2023 to better understand perspectives on youth participation at key decision-making tables where decisions are made that affect our lives and our planet.

Pioneered in partnership with The Possibilists and the Vienna University of Economics and Business, this novel research has the goal to identify global recommendations and collaborative frameworks for generations to come.

The study demographics included 996 individuals from 104 countries. The age range was between 14 and 74 years old, with an average age of 31 years old. This study covered 57 different industries.

Three Key Insights from the Collaborating Across Generations Report:

- 96% believe intergenerational collaboration holds significant value and can generate positive change.
- 87% recognize the powerful potential of youth ideas and solutions in addressing global challenges.
- 72% believe organizations are NOT empowering young people to contribute their unique perspectives.

I experienced youthwashing on many different levels. For example, many times I have been asked to rewrite speeches more than once to be more "gentle and inspirational only." Even though I had been invited to attend and speak at these platforms, I still felt like I was an item on their checklist:

- young
- female
- person of color
- from a developing country
- but can speak fluent English

Before we go any further, it is probably useful to remind each other that stereotyping gets us nowhere.

Keeping an open mind is one of the key elements to a successful intergenerational collaboration. We must avoid the fear of being rejected or stereotyped because it doesn't create a space for intentional learning and growth.

So, how do we prevent youthwashing & Push for intergenerational collaboration?

Do we just stop working together? NO! Connecting young people with CEOs and the other way around is so powerful, as it begins to create intergenerational-led change. Reverse mentorship has incredible value for both parties to learn something new.

This learning opportunity is what we create with YOUTHTOPIA and our SHIFT program – recognize the differences of each generation and use that as our strength for collaborations. It doesn't have to be something that divides us.

LESSON #69: GIVE, GO, OFFER (THE GO WITH 2 G'S)

These three points can be seen as a "starting point" on how to prevent youthwashing. I like to call it:

Go with 2 G's

1) Give us the stage. Young people have a message, and we deserve to be represented on these platforms. Invite us and hear our message, but pay close attention to the following points because this is where it counts:
2) Go a step further than just the stage and involve us in the "behind the scenes" process. We want to get involved backstage too and understand the process! There is a before and after element here.

BEFORE: Involve us in the event planning or the campaign strategy. We want to contribute our ideas before it rolls out!

AFTER: Allow us to be your best implementers. We can accelerate and distribute information like no previous generation. Let us help with the implementation of your goals.

3) Offer us resources and opportunities. This could be mentorship programs or funding opportunities. We may be young and have less experience than some of the other experts in the field, but our ideas and our time and energy should be properly compensated (as I shared about in chapter five in regard to our speaking agency for young changemakers with the London Speaker Bureau).

Once you see those three actions are taken, the next lesson gets put into practice.

LESSON #70: OUR DIFFERENCES CAN BE OUR STRENGTHS

Establishing a sense of mutual respect for our differences sets the tone for a successful collaboration. Understand that there may be different approaches to how we tackle challenges, and also understand that our skill sets could be polar opposites.

LESSON #71: THE POWER OF MENTORS

We still have so much to learn, and we can learn from each other. We also know that we cannot do it alone. So, where us young people have the passion and the vision, the other generations have experience, knowledge, networking, and resources that we have not even begun to collect because we simply haven't had the time nor opportunity to prove ourselves.

At 22, I found myself in a really unique position. I already had a 10-plus-year track record behind me, having started at 12 years old. My skills in public speaking, networking, government relations, managing a team, hiring and firing, and time management were at a very high level for my age group. But I knew I still had a lot to learn, like how to navigate partnerships and create a sustainable business model that actually makes money so I can keep doing this work. You know...just the average things you start questioning when you start your own thing.

IMPROVEMENT. EXPERIENCE. LEARNING.

That is where the power of mentors comes in! I've learned so much from my mentors and advisors. Their guidance has shaped me to become who I am today. I've looked up to them, challenged them, and there were also times where I disagreed with them entirely. But that's the golden stuff. And I'd like to think that through this intergenerational discourse and support, the Baby Boomers feel the benefit just as much as we do.

- Who is in your community doing similar things that you can learn from?
- Look outside of your community, explore the different cultures and global reach.
- Look outside of your work, look for someone in a different field using different skills who you feel might benefit your goal.

LESSON #72-77: THE DO'S & DON'T FOR FINDING A MENTOR

Once you've identified your dream mentor(s), it is time to reach out! This message requires a thoughtful and respectful approach. So, I've listed three "do's" and three "don't" for you to keep in mind when you craft this outreach message!

The 3 Do's

#72: DO YOUR RESEARCH

- **Understand Their Work**: Before reaching out, ensure you know about their professional background, achievements, and contributions. This signals to them that you did your homework and know what you are talking about, but also it shows them respect and genuine interest.
- **Identify Common Interests**: Highlight any common interests or connections you share to create a more personal and relevant request.

#73: BE CLEAR AND SPECIFIC

- **Purpose of Mentorship**: Clearly explain why you are seeking their mentorship and what you hope to achieve from the relationship.
- **Specific Requests**: Outline specific areas where you need guidance. What exactly are you asking for mentorship on? Whether it's career advice, skill development, or project feedback, be clear!

#74: SHOW APPRECIATION & FOLLOW UP

- **Express Gratitude**: Start by appreciating their work and explaining how it has impacted you. This doesn't only set a personal tone, it also shows you value their expertise.
- **Thank Them for Their Time**: As busy changemakers ourselves, we know that time is valuable! Acknowledge that they have busy schedules and express gratitude for considering your request.
- **Keep Them Updated**: Share updates on your progress and how their advice has helped you. This helps maintain the relationship and shows that you value their guidance!

The 3 Don'ts

#75: DON'T BE VAGUE

- **Avoid General Requests**: Don't send a generic request for mentorship. Be specific about why you are reaching out to them and what you hope to gain.

- **Don't Expect Immediate Answers**: Understand that they may need time to consider your request, and don't press for an immediate response.

#76: DON'T OVERWHELM THEM

- **Limit Your Requests**: Don't ask for too much too soon. Start with small, manageable requests and build from there.
- **Respect Their Boundaries**: If they set boundaries around their availability, respect those limits.

#77: DON'T MAKE IT ALL ABOUT YOU

- **Consider Their Perspective**: A mentorship relationship is a two-way street. Show interest in their experiences and insights.
- **Offer to Help**: If you think this would be applicable, offer ways you can assist them, whether through projects or other contributions.

Mentorship and working together across generations is one of the ways I think we will scale solutions everywhere. The collaboration opportunities are huge! I know there is still a lot of heartache and miscommunication when it comes to understanding our differences as generations, but working together will only be beneficial for both sides, on both a personal and professional level.

However, and this is a big however, the collaboration across generations will only be a success if the partnership is built on a strong foundation. But how do we get a strong foundation?

LESSON #78: HOW TO ESTABLISH A GOOD COLLABORATION

One of my favorite examples of a great collaboration is between Greenpeace and Studio Birthplace.

Greenpeace & Studio Birthplace

Greenpeace is a massive, independent global campaigning network, founded in Canada in 1971 by a group of activists. They are mostly known for their non-violent confrontation to expose global environmental problems and develop solutions for a green and peaceful future.

Studio Birthplace is a creative studio telling the Earth's most urgent stories. They are mostly known for their incredible creative ways to bring a message forward with their films, from plastic pollution to the rigged financial systems and their connection to the climate crisis.

Two organizations with the same end goal of creating a better world but with very different avenues of getting there. One through confrontation in action, and the other through confrontation in films. A match made in heaven, as they say. When put together, Greenpeace brought the strength of a large, well-recognized movement while Studio Birthplace supplied the superpowers of creativity. From here, you end up with super unique campaigns like the one called Wasteminster. Imagine watching a video of a digital world featuring Downing Street in the UK, with a mannequin version of Boris Johnston giving a speech. Suddenly, plastic starts raining down from the sky, taking over the screen as a massive wave of plastic cascades through the streets of London. You can imagine how these really strong, never-before-seen images helped boost the exciting potential of new momentum for an old message.

Shifting from media, it is also really important to create physical places to come together in collaboration. That is exactly what the Children and Youth pavilion has done!

Children & Youth Pavilion at COP Conferences

Conference of Parties, or mostly referred to as COP, is the United Nations Framework Convention on Climate Change (UNFCCC) – an international meeting focusing on climate. COP is the main decision-making body of the UNFCCC.

Children and youth have been attending COP conferences for years to learn, to share, and to act a critical reminder that time is ticking! As of COP27 (27 years into the conference's existence), it was finally established that young people would have our very own pavilion! Alongside countries and private sector pavilions, young people now had our very own space. This showcases us as key stakeholders and signals to everyone that we are now included as a serious partner.

All programs at the Children and Youth pavilion at COP conferences are led by the youth, for the youth. Its aim is to amplify the voices of young people and drive action on global climate policies vital to securing our future. By putting different generations together in a normally very rigid setting, this collaboration shows the possibility of what can happen when we work together.

YOUTHTOPIA Shift

On a more personal and long-term level, at YOUTHTOPIA, we have created programs for corporations to engage in. This came about after I started recognizing something interesting. I learned that the students were not alone in asking how to start creating change. This question of where to start often came up in boardrooms and annual meetings as well. CEOs and general managers would come up to me and ask, "Melati, what next steps should we take? Where do we go from here?"

Instead of pretending to have all the answers, YOUTHTOPIA created a program "Changemakers to the Boardrooms." In short, this program puts everything we discussed in this chapter into practice. Reverse mentorship, collaboration across generations, etc. We do this by identifying the expert changemakers within each industry and pair them with the organization/institution that is asking for help.

COLLABORATE. MOTIVATE. ELEVATE.

- **Define Clear Outcomes**

Identifying this from the start will save you so much hassle back and forth in the future. The clear outcome of the partnership, whether it be project-based with a deadline or indefinite, will be your guiding north star.

- **Define Roles and Responsibilities**

I'm a big fan of cheering people on for what they do well. Recognizing our strengths, not only as individuals but as organizations, will allow the collaboration to thrive. Do not become each other and don't compete: stick to your differences and come together to make something new.

- **Timeline with Goals**

Clarity and focus within a timeline always helps everyone keep motivated. Create short- and long-term goals. Assign deadlines and regularly hold check-in meetings.

Sometimes it can seem a bit unusual at first to create collaborations that are inviting others across industries or expertise. But now more than ever, we need to welcome those cultural differences and diverse perspectives. Working together, we can accelerate in our mission to make the world a better place.

CHAPTER EIGHT:

EGO, SELF-LOVE, LEADERSHIP

Lessons in this chapter:

#79: Don't let your ego take lead
#80: Honesty is the best policy
#81: Accept where you are right now
#82: Beware of burnout
#83: "It is a privilege to burn out"
#84: Stop being busy just to be busy
#85: You don't always have to have an answer
#86: Take care of your energy

A poem written in 2022
I was 21 years old

Sometimes my mind is
So
So
So
LOUD
I think I might cause an earthquake
But other days it causes me to smile,
till I cry
And other days my thinking feels like magic
In fact, it's so magical
it becomes hard to translate
And so most days
I sit inside of my mind
thinking: what do I have to do
with all this…
Thinking

Let's talk about ego.

I hate that it still feels like a taboo subject, when we literally all have an ego side within. Especially when you're still in the phase of developing yourself, it is only normal to listen to it. And look at the world we have built around us – it is expected that we have an ego. We built a society that values your followers over your questions. It celebrates you for your earnings vs. your contributions to society. It's a credit and value system that literally is designed to feed your ego. It's the story of ME vs. WE.

What is an ego?

Did you know that the Latin word for ego is "I"? It was the psychologist Sigmund Freud (well, actually his original translator) who put ego into the popular vocabulary, but what he meant by the word is complex, so only other psychologists really use it in the Freudian sense. The rest of us generally use ego simply to mean one's sense of self-worth, whether exaggerated or not.

So, for example, if a person seems to begin every sentence with "I", it's sometimes a sign of a big ego. So far in this book, the word "I" has been used roughly 1,460 times. Is that a lot? Not sure. However, in conversations and in speeches onstage, I know it is an active and conscious decision to not start too many sentences with the word "I."

I'm mindful about this after I heard a speech of a founder, and the word "I" was used way too many times. It ticked me off so much! Halfway through the speech, it was almost funny; so I had to start counting.

Does ego belong in activism?

Well, I'm not sure if it belongs in activism, but it certainly is there. I'm sure we all know a handful of changemakers in the movement who, let's just say, takes up a lot of *space*.

For the longest time, I was in denial, too. I hated it when someone would call me out on my ego. Because *no way, not me!* But the more I have learned to accept that my ego is there, I feel that it no longer guides me forward. It doesn't make my decisions for me. Of course, there is still a lot I have to learn.

Me. Vs. We.

What I have learned so far, though, is that oftentimes, the people who accuse you the hardest of having an ego are the ones who have one big, fat ego themselves. When people call you out, and are almost angry and mad while doing it, they're really frustrated that they aren't the ones in your position. This can be really hard to handle, especially for those of us who are in this fight for everything except ourselves. It's frustrating when these hurdles of ego are so small compared to everything that really matters.

I've also learned that the egomaniac character can also be the source of our problems. It is the very idea of Me vs. We.

So, is ego bad? Personally, I don't think it is all evil. But it definitely cannot be the center of how you make all your decisions. Acknowledge its presence, but do not allow it to become or make decisions for you.

LESSON #79: DON'T LET YOUR EGO TAKE LEAD

The times my ego took over

When I started working with companies, contracts became involved. It changed the entire dynamic of what we were doing and *how* we were doing things. And if I am being really honest, for a moment there, it also questioned *why* we were doing this work.

At 12 years old, I had practically created a workflow where I was my own boss. Suddenly, that wasn't the case anymore with these contracts. There were a handful of instances along the years where I have let my ego get me in trouble.

Oftentimes, I am eager and quick to get collaborations started, especially with companies who show a real promise to change their direction and prioritize sustainability.

Because of this eagerness, one of my first mistakes I made was signing a contract that wasn't complete or clear. This would later bite me in the butt. It had the overall intention and idea of the outcomes, but without the numbers behind it. For example, the missing information related to time, duration, publication, platform, etc.

As young changemakers we are often told, "We want to work with you and make sure you are happy with this collaboration just as much as we are." Whenever I heard this, I thought: *How nice of them, we can grow together. An innovative team, a future-proof company.*

And then, the working collaboration started, and I ignored the vague contract and continued with trust. *It will be fine.*

In some cases, it does work out where everyone comes out of the collaboration happy. In other cases, it starts to become a real headache. I've had a few instances where a working collaboration worked out perfectly for the first few months, and then slowly, expectations and outcomes became blurry.

After a few points were ticked off on the contract, I would suddenly find myself doing more than agreed. And this is what many of us changemakers experience when we play with the corporate world. We do the videos, we do the consultancy work, but then, there is always that one or two (or three) extra things that are expected to be brushed off.

In my case, this example came in the form of an internal gathering to meet the leaders of the company. It was one of those things that wasn't on the contract but encouraged by partners to do to "maintain the relationship." This is a funny concept created by the adult world. It's called networking and showing face. It's a surface-level connection that signals to them that you're willing to play the same game they do.

Thinking I didn't have any other option and without knowing any better, I said okay. I traveled a whole day there and back. The meeting was pleasant: it was exactly what you'd expect. A private room for lunch where they ordered way too much food. I kept thinking, *There will be so much food waste.* The conversation was polite, and it was good to meet the team.

When we walked out of the lunch room and got into cars to head to their HQ, I thought my involvement was done. But I had a bad feeling that they were thinking the exact opposite. I was right. "So Melati, it's just something small, you will be our guest of honor," they said. For an "oh-it's-nothing" event, I was shocked that they had so many printed materials. Posters with my name on it, and photographers ready to capture the sound bites for social media. To say I felt uncomfortable is an understatement.

They said it was just a small thing, internal only so I shouldn't make a big fuss out of it. In reality, it was a free, 45-minute "Melati, please be inspiring" session that they didn't want to recognize as a contract item.

From that moment on, I created this idea in my head that they weren't worth the hassle. It didn't matter what I did or gave them, they would take way more than what was agreed anyway. It was unfair and annoying. But what was really going on was my ego was hurt.

I was hurt that I got myself in this situation in the first place. *How stupid am I*? I thought to myself. *I should've known better.*

But here I was, in a situation where there were still a few items contractually pending from my side. And I decided to go M.I.A.

I didn't want to send those items because I thought they already got a fair share of deliverables. But who am I to think like that? *Melati Melati Melati.*

I was in a lot of trouble, and agents were getting involved at this point because I had just simply stopped answering emails. They were using rough language, and I was starting to feel pretty bad. I turned to my mama and told her how I felt.

She listened and responded with, "You feel bad because you know you are wrong. And I know you don't like it when people tell you that you made a mistake, but this time, you messed up. It's a good lesson for you on how the big people world works, Melati. The world doesn't turn for you, sweetie. Business is business."

She's right. She's always right.

That very next Monday, I went into the office and focused all of my attention on finishing the contract items. I changed the team working on it, set time aside myself, and put forth a new timeline. Finally, I wrote them an email saying, "I'm sorry".

It felt like a big weight lifted off my shoulders. Being honest to yourself and to others is always the best way forward. You can do anything you set out to achieve, and you learn even more when you fix the hurdles ahead of you instead of ignoring them and hiding behind your ego.

LESSON #80: HONESTY IS THE BEST POLICY

During the ten years of being a changemaker, a founder, a face on the front lines, I have had many moments that fanned my ego to grow. I've opened the stage for President Barack Obama in a stadium with 9,000 people. I've climbed the elite and famous steps of the red carpet of the Cannes Film Festival in a dress tailored and specially designed for me by Indonesia's leading designer. The world of a 12-year-old island girl quickly grew into a global, fancy playground. It is easy to get lost in the glitz and the glam.

But each moment can teach you something about yourself and your ego.

It also taught me a lot about how we have to change the narrative: we may all be in the same storm, but we are definitely not all in the same boat, as Vanessa Nakate has said. How do we blend these different privileges and levels of leadership to benefit the larger movement of change? How do we not leave anybody behind?

This I experienced firsthand, when I met one of the world's biggest leaders.

Opening for President Barack Obama

It was an email that came into my inbox late one evening. I was just about to close my laptop and call it a night when the notification popped up.

URGENT: Melati onstage with PBO?

Here is what my thought process looked like:

Urgent? What stage could be so urgent? And finally,

Who the hell is PBO?

P B O....?

It took me a good five minutes and a Google search before I almost fell off my chair.

President. Barack. Obama.

I laughed hysterically because I thought it was spam. There was no way this could be real. Right? A nobody from Bali? To open for a former president? This was HUGE! Imagine all the people this message would reach. This was the next step for me in my career!!

I ran out of the office without locking the doors that evening. I changed clothes immediately when I got home and put my running shoes on and put my earphones in. I needed to run. I needed to think. I needed to be present and absorb this moment. This invitation. As I started to run, it began to rain. I could feel the fresh tropical raindrops falling. I could have turned around and stayed home. Instead, I continued and ran in the rain. I danced in the rain. I said thank you in the rain.

The next day, I was in the plane and arrived hours before I would open for Mr. PBO.

I remember being baffled by the stadium. It was my biggest stage to date. It was also one of my first solo trips. And while I had the help of Hans, the person who had put my name forward, and friends and family who had traveled to Amsterdam to watch, I felt very nervous before it started, doubting if I was the right person.

The theme was ***leadership***. At this point, I had led Bye Bye Plastic Bags for 10 years, and YOUTHTOPIA was entering its 3rd year under my lead. But the thing is, I didn't think I was a leader at all. When calling with my mom, she said it too. *Great, Mum, thanks. That's exactly what I needed to hear right now.*

But she also said this: "It's not about you. You have a gift to inspire other people with your words and your story and your energy. Be YOU and do what you do best, but take off the pressure because it isn't about you, it's about what you can do."

No, I was not a leader yet. At least, I knew I hadn't reached my full potential. But I was learning, and I was confident enough to go out there because there is a difference between confidence and ego.

The moment I decided it wasn't about me, I suddenly had confidence. I could stand taller, I could walk smoother, my heart rate slowed, and I got on that stage to do what I can do best: share a story that is bigger than all of us but needs every single one of us.

BUT, here's the thing: we've built a culture around us where we need to have that leader. That one face who we can say "it's because of you."

"It's because of you we are here today."

"It's because of you that we managed to get another investment."

"It's because of you that the company/school/project is a success."

And, don't get me wrong, this one face doesn't only get the praise; it also holds the weight of the responsibility. When things go wrong, it's a lot easier to blame one person instead of a group of people.

"It's your fault we didn't make it to the final round."

"It was your ego that let the partnership fall through."

"It's you who didn't prepare well."

It's the top of the ladder, the top of the food chain. It's for the ones who win the survival of the fittest. The kings of the jungle. And it's not for the faint of heart.

The Lion, The Sheep, The Zebra...

We have created a culture where we celebrate the lion and laugh at the sheep. I was at a school presentation one day when I heard a speaker ask the roomful of students to chant:

"Be a lion, don't be a sheep."

"Be a lion, don't be a sheep."

"Be a lion, don't be a sheep."

And another speaker told the kids:

"You need more energy! Act like you are happy, and then you will feel it."

But the thing with all of this is that it builds an insane amount of pressure. It's an insanely high bar. Even when we are adults standing on our tippy toes, we will feel society's expectations of us are so far out of reach. AND WHY? Why do we put ourselves through this? Why do we paint this end goal that is so impossible?

What if you don't want to be a lion? So what if you are a sheep? Or what if you want to be a zebra? Or an elephant? It's beyond crazy that we still associate the meaning of a leader to be equivalent to the faces at the front of the movement. Obama is only the person he is because of his team and the people he has around him: the tech engineers working backstage, the marketing team, the ticketing and guest welcoming team. Without any of them, the show would have been a nightmare. We need an entire jungle. And a healthy jungle has all biodiversity living in harmony with each other. Not just lions.

And about the emotions: there is too much pressure on us to feel good all the time. To feel happy or to be bright and to be excellent. All. The. Time.

LESSON #81: ACCEPT WHERE YOU ARE RIGHT NOW

It is exhausting to be switched "on" in a world that doesn't sleep. We create a culture of "fake it till you make it" until we forget reality. We forget to feel. We grow so distant from ourselves that we don't even know what we are feeling anymore. We grow numb. And this is where the problem starts, the disconnection to the world we live in and to the people around us. We need to learn how to accept where we are right now.

When it was my turn to lead a workshop, I felt the challenge of creating that space for us to accept our feelings. I wanted to change the energy in the room. The chairs were in rows, one line after the other. There was no possibility for connection with one another. I asked the students for their help. They picked up their chairs and made a circle. Over 60 students sat in a circle, and I could watch them slowly look around, acknowledging each other. *Much better.*

To start off, I asked the same students who chanted "I am a lion" a simple question.

My question was this;

"Can I see a show of hands, everyone here who has heard of the term anxiety?"

All hands went up. Next question:

"Keep your hands up if you've personally experienced anxiety before."

Without a flinch, all hands stayed up.

Every single one.

The air was still, and nobody moved. Together, we all held our breath.

I was shocked that a roomful of teens had already experienced so much anxiety. I knew anxiety was common amongst our generation, but this was not okay, every single person in this room admitted to experiencing it before. A weight traveled down to the pit of my stomach. *How can this be?*

What do I do now? As the host of this workshop, I suddenly felt the anxiety myself. I wasn't trained for a situation like this. But I quickly tapped into my own feelings and remembered one of the most important lessons.

"Take a look around the room." I said, slowly releasing my breath. With their hands still up in the air, everyone looked quietly around the room.

"You are not alone. It is okay to feel this way. It is normal to feel this way about the world we live in."

In that moment, I felt our shoulders collectively drop. We melted from a space of singularity to a group of one. It was like this workshop was the space students were craving for all day long. Questions and interaction, their potential peeked out of their shyness, and I could see that slowly and together, we were redefining what it meant to be a leader.

You are not alone.

LESSON #82: BEWARE OF BURNOUT

We've become very focused on the end goal, and yet, along the way, we lose sight of the end goal. There is an idea as to why this happens, and it had to do with what happens internally. To understand this, let me introduce…

Inner Development Goals: a nonprofit, open-source initiative committed to fostering inner development towards more sustainable futures. The idea is that we won't achieve any of the 17 Sustainable Development Goals without first doing the much needed Inner Development work. In many ways, I think this is true, and this work calls for us all to normalize creating space for reflection and celebration. Work on ourselves, our understanding of the world, and the responsibility we each carry.

But this unfortunately is not the norm, and because it is not, we have created very easy and unhealthy cycles to fall into. Cue the climate anxiety, the emotional overwhelm of everyday decision-making, the distraction of the ego...the list goes on.

Why do we continue to create a pace for ourselves that we cannot keep up with? It is a constant challenge against the status quo. Knowing how to navigate your ego and anxiety and what is happening to our environment go hand in hand. Not educating ourselves only fuels the already-underlying uncertainty.

The burnout

For nearly three years in a row, I would burn out by September of each year. I tried everything, but no matter what I did, it had become my "burnout month." I'd worked so hard, or one could argue, so blindly, from the start of each year to the burnout month ... and I just felt like giving up.

According to a study from Cigna Survey, Gen Z is the most stressed-out generation. Nearly all Gen Z workers (98%) are battling burnout symptoms, with 23% saying that they experience "unmanageable stress" and 48% reporting that they feel drained.

I felt like the work we were doing was not enough, so I started to ask these types of questions:

What does it matter anyway? Nothing will change.

Who cares if we say no to one single use item? It's just one dumb plastic bag.

What difference will it even make? The world is dying.

This was the sign of my burnout starting: loss of hope. It is a very hard place to turn around from. If the feeling of burnout is like carrying a rock up a hill only to drop it back down, losing hope is the feeling of being stuck in a dark hole in the center of the world, with absolutely no vision of how to get yourself back out. The worst part about this is when you realize you are the one holding the shovel, digging yourself deeper and deeper. That moment really sucks. And I know at this point, we are supposed to say something uplifting like:

"But, hey! At least you are the one doing it to yourself, so you can also get out of it!"

"If there was a way in, there is a way out!"

"You got this."

But honestly, maybe because it's the mood I am in when I'm writing this, but I just want to sit here for a second and collectively create space to say:

Burnouts suck.

Every time I've experienced a burnout, it ruins and steals something deeper within me. When I feel hopeless, it gets harder and harder to find myself again.

I cry a lot.

I feel a lot.

It just really, really sucks.

The end.

Gotcha! Don't worry, I wouldn't leave you hanging like that. Of course there is more…

Conversation with Mohamad Al Jounde on burnout

We were on another Zoom webinar, in the thick of the pandemic, and we were talking about burnouts. I asked, "Can we avoid burnout? Or is it inevitable?"

The face on the other side of the screen looked tired and aged. Mohamad, my dear friend who I met while filming *Bigger Than Us*, paused briefly before he answered my question. He unmuted his microphone and said, "I think all activists should go through a burnout at one point in their journey. We have to change the way we look at that moment in life. It may be the lowest moment, but through that experience, only then are we truly faced with the most important question: why am I doing this work?"

There are a series of questions that most activists should be confronted with, he continued, "Without a burnout, we might not know our real reason. Are you doing this for yourself? To get more followers? Are you doing this work to get rich? Or are you doing this because you really want to help? If you know your real "why," it helps you build resilience and keep on going."

Here's the thing: most of the time, quick fixes don't work. Wait, let me try that again: quick fixes *don't* work, *ever.* That's the *brutal, honest truth.*

In my moments of burnout, I was desperate. I wanted to find the magic formula that would make me *better*, so I did a lot of quick fixes. I did not want to feel this hopeless. I did not want to feel this stuck. I thought that was not what activists feel. I wanted to cry.

2019 Burnt-Out Melati

I went to Oneworld Ayurveda, a wonderful space focusing on natural health and healing. I stayed there for a whole week. Seven days of healthy food, two massages daily, a yoga class in the mornings, and absolutely no work. Sounds like heaven, right? On the first night I checked in, I cried myself to sleep and remembered not knowing what to do with myself and all of this *quiet*.

2020 Burnt-Out Melati

In the height of the pandemic, I created a series where we talked about our mental health, with the hope that if we talk about it, maybe something would change.

2021 Burnt-Out Melati

Turns out, talking about it didn't do so much for me. So this round, I tried the exact opposite of talking. I went to a silent retreat and didn't speak for 10 days. I cried the most here and ended up losing 10 kilograms over two months.

LESSON #83: "IT IS A PRIVILEGE TO BURN OUT"

I heard this phrase once, and it changed the way I viewed burnouts. Some people simply do not have the privilege to take time out to analyze their burnout. They have to keep on going because their family depends on them or their financial situation requires it of them.

There is so much we do not see. It is a privilege to be able to rest when you need to; it is a privilege to be able to go on these retreats.

It frustrates me that this is another norm that we somehow have allowed to happen. **As if rest is anything but a human right.** Rest isn't earned. Rest is a right.

I've tried to follow the 5 Rules to keep me in check from burnout:

Rest Reconnect Reevaluate Reintegrate Redo

Rest

The very first step is to take yourself out of the busy hustle and just do nothing. Oftentimes, my resting spots are deep in nature.

Reconnect

When you're in the zone of rest, find the time to reconnect with yourself and what brings you joy.

Reevaluate

When you're in this content, rested, and reconnected zone, you are able to create the space you need to reevaluate your situation. *Why* did you end up here? What is important to you?

Reintegrate

Now, you've found your focus once again. You've listened to yourself. Hopefully, this gives you an energized feeling of being ready to reintegrate back into the "real world" again.

Redo

This is easy to forget, but arguably the most important aspect. Practicing the above once doesn't work for long-lasting change. **Again, there is no quick, onetime fix. This is the practice of a lifetime.** This is a healthy and "should be normal" way of moving through life.

The key element is to not let yourself go too long without the first R before the burnout takes its roots deep within. Make time for that rest, reconnect, reevaluate, and then reintegrate. And on a regular basis, do it all over again: redo!

But it isn't always that easy. Slowly and all at once, inside of my mind, I started to hear a question. A voice inside kept repeating: when are you going to stop running? When are you going to allow yourself to just rest?

LESSON #84: STOP BEING BUSY JUST TO BE BUSY

There is so much expectation around change, but especially towards individual changemakers: the people who are working in this space. The question, "What's next, Melati?" used to excite me, until it became the literal cause for so much of my anxiety. What's next?

I don't know.

This is a statement I would never admit out loud. I'd always come up with something because there was always *something I was doing*. It's true, I was making myself busier and busier just to feel like I was busy. Doing *something*. Another talk, another campaign, another government rally. I was doing a lot, but the feeling of emptiness, of nothingness, would start to grow inside, all hope and purpose gone.

That is the moment you start to turn into someone you don't recognize. Again, you feed from a place of exhaustion and the belief that you need to keep on going. It goes back to the topic about ego and the lesson of not doing things because you think you have to, but only because you want to. This belief that without you, the whole world will stop spinning. Stop being busy just to be busy.

It is a privilege to be asked: "What's next, Melati?"

So today, in those moments, when someone asks me, "What's next, Melati?" instead of instantly following the knee-jerk reaction to answer with the next big project, I give myself a moment to recognize everything that has already been achieved up until this very moment. I try to feel the pride and all the hard work that has gone into being here. And then sometimes…

LESSON #85: YOU DON'T ALWAYS HAVE TO HAVE AN ANSWER

Accept the place in between: the magic of wondering "where to next?"

Melati vs. YOUTHTOPIA > the founder syndrome?

Sometimes, lingering in that magical place in between not having an answer is harder than we think. Whether I like it or not, the media at-large has painted me to be the face of my organization. So, naturally, this was a common reaction whenever I suggested someone else go in my place. "No, they want you, Melati."

My body would literally have an allergic reaction whenever I heard that. *No, they don't understand. I am just one person. YOUTHTOPIA is so many more of us.* For years, I tried to build YOUTHTOPIA to be the movement of young changemakers. Finally, a big enough platform of protection to stand behind. I was done being the face of Bye Bye Plastic Bags. The last thing I wanted was to become the face of YOUTHTOPIA. It defeated the entire point of why YOUTHTOPIA exists. There isn't one person or one project that can solve the challenges we are in. We need all of us.

That is the power of a community. We celebrate the diversity of all of us. It's a beautiful thing, don't you think? And here I am, a young founder at the front lines of change, holding the headlines of the media too. It's a lot of pressure. And a tight dance. And not a sustainable one at all.

It was a series of questions from my mentors that made me start to shift as a young, full-time changemaker and founder. My mentor, Chris, proposed this question to me that I didn't think to spend much time on before:

"What happens to your company if you die tomorrow?"

Another one of my mentors, Matthew, asked me:

"Do you feel that you've built YOUTHTOPIA to be able to run without you on a daily basis?"

I didn't like the answer for either question. I realized this was another challenge I fell into. The media is a big monster in this system, shaping so many of the narratives that eventually shape who we are. For so long, movements are celebrated by the few faces at the front; but our generation is changing that.

We know that this narrative of one only fuels competition in a world that desperately needs more collaboration. We urgently need to change our culture from competition to collaboration.

LESSON #86: TAKE CARE OF YOUR ENERGY

All of this outer-world anxiety started to translate how I treated my inner world. I'm a bit embarrassed to admit that I let my relationship with food slip. I'm not really sure if I remember when it all began, but I started to believe that I was only deserving to eat if I had been productive enough. I'm not proud of it. It has been something I have actively worked hard to make better – disassociating the feeling of guilt with reward.

Guilt is a learned feeling. We are not born knowing what guilt feels like.

The end of the day: food is fuel. You need to eat. The chase for enough is an illusion. You are enough.

I try as much as possible to look back at these lessons and see the positive side of what they have taught me. I learned about balance and about regeneration, which perhaps could be the final R of the Rest, Reconnect, Revaluate, Reintegrate, and Redo. Regeneration builds a strong foundation for long-term change. Regeneration is, like sustainability, becoming more and more a buzzword. Intuitively, we may understand that it means putting back in more than we take from the world, while at the same time, fixing the damage that our economic systems have caused to the natural world. Essentially, it goes one step further than sustainability and is an entirely new level of ambition that reaches a new paradigm shift.

But back to the topic at hand, paradigm-building is no easy task. It takes a lot of courage, self-reflection, global leadership… and that's just the beginning.

So, regeneration is a goal internally, as well as externally.

This part is ironically the hardest. Because at least on an internal and personal level, there is comfort in playing the victim. There is no responsibility in that world. But it is also a reflection of why and how we have allowed the world to come to such a dying state. I have now come to realize that practicing "self care" directly links to "we care," and in turn, directly links to planetary health. Without a healthy population, both mentally and physically, we are not able to take care of the planet or each other. It's as simple as that. "You cannot pour from an empty cup." Regenerate yourself to regenerate the movement.

I once saw this interview of an entrepreneur being asked this question: "What's the biggest lie you've ever been told?"

In one swift breath, he answered, "It's not that simple."

The reporter started to probe him on, "But if you had to choose one lie, what would it...?"

The entrepreneur interrupted him to say, "No, you don't understand. I mean, that was the biggest lie I've ever been told: that it's not that simple. **It is.**"

CHAPTER NINE:

THE HEART, THE MIND, THE SYSTEMS

Lessons in this chapter:

#87: Set yourself up for success
#88: Keep a diverse group around you
#89: Dating (as) a changemaker
#90: Practice self-love
#91: You are not your passport
#92: Systems are designed to fail us
#93: Use the system to work for us

A poem written in 2022
I was 21 years old

Lost sounded like a
foreign feeling once
I remember someone first
describing it to me
Lost
And I thought, what a silly concept,
to not know
where you are
To not know
Who you are
I was so confidently naive
I thought,
Lost,
Not me!
But perhaps there is a new lost that nobody told me about
The type of lost that you don't know about
Until you've found yourself
loose
in
being
lost

LESSON #87: SET YOURSELF UP FOR SUCCESS

At some point, 7:35 a.m. coffees at the local corner shop became a routine. Every week, I would meet up with one of my "biggest box" friends, Jord. A life-coach-turned-friend-for-life who mentored and saw me through some of my worst pain points and celebrated me through many of my biggest personal and professional achievements. Before I explain the concept of big box friends, I thought I'd explain the whole "7:35 a.m."

I realized that I needed to set myself up for success, but I needed a little help. Every time we agreed to meet at 7:30 a.m., I would arrive five minutes late because I just needed those extra few minutes of sleep. I felt terrible.

I would run into the cafe, flustered and throwing out an apology for being late. Jord would calmly sit there and smile at me saying, over and over, "It's okay, Melati," followed by a casual, "How'd you sleep?" One morning, he shrugged his shoulders and suggested, "Shall we just aim for 7:35 a.m.?" Little did I know that small gesture would change my life forever. I always made it at 7:35 a.m., and I was never late again. That small move of just acknowledging where you are and what your reality is was a huge reminder that you yourself have the power to create your own success. This is something that only people with worldly thinking and understanding can accommodate to. Let me now explain the "big box theory."

It came up during one of our coffee conversations at the corner store. "We live in a box of comfort. Think about it. We are all born into lives set out for us. But every experience we live through or create adds to our character and way of moving through life."

It's like all of our experiences, all of our friends, all of our memories become collections in our "life box." So, the big box theory means that the more experience you add to your "box," and the more your box expands, the more open-minded and eager you are to find others who have more experience too.

The topic of friends intrigued me when it came to this idea. We talked about different friends that we do different things with. I shared: "I have my party friends, my changemaker friends, my professional partner friends ... is it strange to separate your friends?"

"No, I don't think so."

"But it's interesting to see who you gravitate toward."

It made me think back to the girl who came up to me after a presentation so many years before; the one who had said she found it difficult to talk to her friends about topics that she was passionate about. It made me think about my group of girlfriends on the island compared to my group of changemaker friends all around the world.

Once again, we all need balance in life. **This means balance in friendships too.**

Growing up on the island of Bali, friendships were challenging to sustain. Everybody leaves. It is such a transitional island. People come, people go. Everybody wants Bali until they need to get back to the real world. By the end of middle school, I had decided that putting the energy into making friends just wasn't worth it anymore. Everybody would leave at some point anyway. So what was the point?

It's a harsh reality to come to at that point in life. At any point really, and I do not wish it upon anyone to reach that conclusion.

Because it is always worth it. Connection and friendship with other people is what keeps us alive. It is the foundation. Real friends are there for all versions of you. They cheer you on for your successes, no matter how big or small; and they are also there for you when you need a cry and a hug.

LESSON #88: KEEP A DIVERSE GROUP AROUND YOU

Over the years, I learned that friendships are also hard work. They take time and attention and sometimes, speaking from my own experience, you find yourself in the position of being a bad friend.

With my work bringing me to different parts of the world, I would miss out on big events at home. My friends' birthdays, their surprise engagements and seeing their partner dropping down on one knee, and then I'd miss the more simple things, too, like the regular weekly dinners.

In my experience, being friends with a changemaker means being prepared for their availability in person to be scarce, but loving them anyway. That's definitely not the easiest and not the nicest. I hate that part too. Being a changemaker can lead to becoming the person who is never there, the one who falls out of touch or doesn't know the new people that enter the friend group.

It happens, and it sucks, but you will find your tribe. And when you do, you will know how to show up in a way that matters to you and your friends. I am so lucky that I found my group. It took me a while, but my friends on the island and beyond are my guiding light. They keep me sane and my age. My friends take me out dancing when life gets too serious. They remind me that what I do is "fucking amazing," *and* they will also tell me off when I get too far in my head. We are there for each other, always and no matter what. I wish for everyone to have a hot grandma group like mine.

So our "big box" expands with those we keep close to us, with each friendship widening our own experiences. This is friendship we've been talking about, though: let's jump over to matters of the heart.

LESSON #89: DATING (AS) A CHANGEMAKER

I love deeply, and I love easily. If I wasn't a full-time changemaker, I would probably pride myself in being a full-time lover. I love giving and receiving love. I *love* love. In my short life, I have already experienced otherworldly, *this is it*, kiss-me-in-the-rain-and-everything-fades-away type of love. My first serious relationship started when I was 17 years old. We were together for nearly 5 years. We did everything together. We grew with each other and for each other, until we started to grow apart from each other.

Being with another changemaker as a partner comes with its

challenges, but for the most part, he was the best first love I could have ever asked for.

We moved in together on our second anniversary, just as the pandemic took over the world. Our home was in the middle of the rice fields with a big garden. We had a dog and two cats. We were so lucky. And in a world we thought was changing too slowly, we decided to go fast. We moved quickly. The world around us saw that. We were, to the outside world, a dynamic duo, the "it" couple, the eco-warriors in love.

We shared a wonderful moment in time together, and I will forever be grateful for our time as partners.

Now, I know there were many things I could have done better. I am still learning a lot, but these are the things I've realized over the years.

Things that worked for us

- We shared the same passions.
- We each had a successful career.
- We could understand what the other person was going through.

Both of us were young founders growing our own companies at the same time as growing a life together – what a beautiful and challenging task that requires balance, patience, and deep understanding. I found that balance became harder the busier we got. Life just got loud. Small changes started happening that showed a shift in priorities until eventually they just became normal.

Red flags in dating a changemaker (or anyone, really)

Jealousy

And no, unfortunately it's not even the jealousy of the usual dating scene. I'm not talking about another girl or guy giving your partner attention, I'm talking about millions of people, the media, the invitations, the awards. Being a changemaker in a relationship, or dating one, means that the whole world is part of it too. There is constantly attention, and there is absolutely no space for jealousy here. You have to be okay – and here I am putting it lightly, because actually you should be happy – that you or your partner is having all of this recognition for your/their work. Be there to support.

Competitiveness

Creating a safe space with no jealousy can be taken to the next level by supporting our partners through collaboration. This might be in ways where active partnerships are formed professionally, or perhaps simply in the small ways of showing up for your partner, completely erasing any space for competition.

Lack of respect for time

You should value the time of your partner just as much as your own time. We all have things to do. It shouldn't be hard to make time for the person you are growing with in life. Setting boundaries here is a must, and talking about when to work and when not to work will prevent the guilt from working.

Manipulative communication

Being clear, honest, and complete builds a strong foundation for trust. Say it like it is and never leave the other person in doubt. And besides, there's a lot on our plates already, having to go onstage or into an interview with a heaviness in your heart just sucks.

Being able to switch on and off

This is a hard one because for most of us, we live and breathe the work that we do. But our partners should also help to create a space where you can just *be*.

When we parted ways, it broke me into a million pieces. I don't know where I would be without my friends and family. They were my lifeline for a good amount of time, every day showing up for me in ways I can't even begin to explain. From emergency sleepovers to flying out to conferences so I wouldn't be alone. It showed me that love comes in so many ways. It's everywhere around you. Love is always there.

Here are 10 things I have learned to look for in a partner. Someone who:

- Brings out the best in you
- Genuinely celebrates you when you achieve your successes
- Is there for you when you fail or just need a shoulder to cry on
- Can listen without rushing to say what they think is important
- Communicates honestly with you
- Doesn't compete with you
- Doesn't want to be with you because of your connections
- You can discuss all topics with
- Creates the space for you to just be YOU
- You can laugh with and have the best time with

Go through life with people who choose YOU.

But at the end of the day, you also have to learn how to choose you. You see, what I came to realize through this whole heartbreak and the heartbreaks after was that I actually had very little love for myself.

LESSON #90: PRACTICE SELF-LOVE

Sometimes self-love can feel like a faraway concept. I think by now, at this point in the book, you've gotten a pretty good feeling of my voice, who I am, and how I think. It took me a while to realize that I had lost touch of "self-love" so much that it started to sound like a fairy tale.

But the truth is, we are all born into the world with a good amount of self-love; nothing would happen without it. When I think back to 12-year-old Melati, that girl only could do what she did from a place deep within, a source of big love. Love for the world around her, but love for herself and the belief she had for what she could do.

So, in my early 20s, I made myself a promise that I would try to find that source of self-love deep within. The burnouts that you read about already definitely didn't help, but at the same time, they pushed me further inside of myself, forcing me to search.

The internal debate

There were moments where I would sit with the question: am I doing enough? *Saying no to single use plastic bags is not going to solve this plastic problem. It is not enough. I am not doing enough. Focusing on education will take too long.* And there the hamster wheel began, and the spin would last days, weeks, months. A very lucid state fueling myself to believe I was not enough.

With persistence and commitment to my promise, slowly, through many practices of mindfulness, dancing, music, writing, and lots of other things I love doing, I finally began to feel grounded in myself again. It also had to do a lot with focusing on the present, practicing gratitude for all that there is, and not feeling the "could of's" of the past or the chase of the future. *I am happy.* And sometimes I am sad, and that is okay because I am at home in myself. The 5 R's of Rest, Reconnect, Reevaluate, Reintegrate, and Redo were on literal repeat.

There is a concept I learned about when I attended a Plum Village retreat on leadership and resilience led by Christiana Figueres and 14 monks of the monastery.

Mindful Walking

Mindful walking is a form of walking meditation that integrates mindfulness into each step. The concept emphasizes being fully present and aware of the act of walking, transforming an everyday activity into a meditative practice. The idea is to synchronize your breath with every step and focus your attention on the sensations in your feet and the movement of the body, bringing your focus to the present.

Mindful walking at Plum Village is not just a physical activity but a practice of cultivating inner peace, mindfulness, and a profound connection to the present moment.

Noble Silence

This practice involves refraining from speaking and engaging in other forms of communication during designated times, typically in the evening and early morning hours. The aim of Noble Silence is to create a serene and contemplative environment, allowing practitioners to deepen their mindfulness and inner peace. It is also a great way to delve deep for some inner reflections.

These practices of aligning your mind, your actions, and your body all help you to pave the pathway forward in a healthy way. When expanding your box and attracting the right people into your life, timing is everything. We know this.

Once you've come back into contact with yourself, your happy place is within YOU; and the right person for you will come along, sometimes when you least expect it. I know they will, mine did. Even though we can be ridiculously hard to handle sometimes, between our frustrations at the larger systems and our busy-changing-the-world schedule…there is that person out there for you who makes you feel extremely loved, cared for, and understood.

Aside from the individual connection we make with one another, there is another source of connection and validation that we look for. This comes from our countries. Our literal identities.

LESSON #91: YOU ARE NOT YOUR PASSPORT

What I am about to share next will make some people mad or sad, or both. We just went through matters of the heart, the mind, and big box people…

Now we dive into the part about "the systems". Opening trigger question:

What happens when the systems don't choose you?

My whole life I thought I was Indonesian. When I was little, I joked about becoming president of our country. Whenever I visited my family in Surabaya, I would always eat my grandmother's soto ayam with extra sambal because "*I am Indonesian.* I can handle it."

I'd sing the anthem, vote in the national elections, stand tall for my passport photos, and find pride in my home country: Indonesia.

But on my 21st birthday, I was told I had never been Indonesian. Ever.

Let me explain.

Dual nationality is a hot topic in Indonesia. We're only entitled to one nationality. For those of us born to two nationalities, we're allowed to keep them until we are 18. Officially, you have to let go of the other nationality at 21 years old as a final decision.

For me, it has always been clear. I knew I wanted to continue doing the work on the ground in Bali and surrounding islands. It was the only decision I had ever let myself entertain. There was no other option. The work, my life, my future: it all belonged right here in Indonesia.

And to set the record straight, I *am* Indonesian. I have a biological Indonesian father, an Indonesian birth certificate and passport since birth. It's all there.

When I turned 21, I was proud to choose my Indonesian nationality. I was finally going to be "*just*" Indonesian.

So, what went wrong?

Apparently in 2006, when there was still no mainstream computer system nor regular postal system in the country, a document called an affidavit was applied for both my sister and I. Today, I know that mine was never completed or lost. Why would my parents have gotten it for one daughter and not the other? It doesn't make sense, so something must have gone wrong.

Administration aside, it never kept me from receiving new Indonesian passports, voting rights, and even a tax number. During international conferences like COP or the World Water Forum, I was always the Indonesian role model and hope for the future, recognized and endorsed by many government leaders from the country. So when I went to proudly confirm my Indonesian nationality at 21 years old, I was shocked when I heard this: "It's complicated, Melati. You don't have the affidavit, *and* you're an activist."

Why had the government not issued a single warning or alert that this was needed in the *years* leading up to this decision?

The additional "*and you're an activist*" attached to the reaction of people felt more and more like a pity statement. My track record as an activist was something that had been celebrated and cheered for my whole life, now it became the very death of my future.

There is this perception globally on what it means to be an activist. The word itself scares some people, "Oh no, not an *activist*." As if Activist translated to a universal code for "danger to the comfort zone." Growing up in Indonesia with a culture of respect towards elders and a generations old belief that girls should not speak up caused me to identify myself as a changemaker and *not* an activist. I had started my work for the positive changes I believe in *for Indonesia*. Yet, there I was, feeling like it had all been a terrible misunderstanding.

LESSON #92: SYSTEMS ARE DESIGNED TO FAIL US

My entire future changed: from one missing document to losing my Indonesian nationality. I was not prepared. Losing my nationality felt like a lot more than losing a passport. The domino effect was intense: it affected my safety, my invitations to high-level government meetings were withdrawn, my ability to publicly speak out and continue doing this activism work was all affected. And to add even more, there was a total and complete personal identity crisis that I was forced into.

Now, unfortunately, this is not a rare occurrence. Many of us around the world have faced repeated and various attempts from our governments to make it harder for us to speak out safely. There are three activist examples that I would like to share to give a deeper perspective:

Activist One: Thich Nhat Hanh

Born Nguyen Xuan Bao in 1926 in central Vietnam, Thich Nhat Hanh was ordained as a monk at the age of 16 at Tu Hieu Temple in Hue, Vietnam. He pioneered the concept of "Engaged Buddhism," emphasizing the application of Buddhist principles to social, political, and environmental issues. He was gaining international recognition within the peace movement.

The Vietnamese government, both in the North and South, saw his actions as a threat to their agendas. This led to Thich Nhat Hanh being exiled from his homeland of Vietnam for over 39 years. Only in 2005 was he was finally able to return.

Activist Two: Benny Wenda

Benny Wenda is a West Papuan independence leader who fled persecution by Indonesian authorities for his role in advocating for West Papuan self-determination. Wenda has been living in exile in the United Kingdom since 2002. He founded the Free West Papua Campaign and is also a founding member of the United Liberation Movement for West Papua.

He continues to raise awareness about human rights abuses and the struggle for independence in West Papua, advocating for international support and recognition of West Papua's right to self-determination.

Activist Three: Wole Soyinka

A Nigerian playwright, novelist, poet, and essayist in the English language, Wole Soyinka was awarded the 1986 Nobel Prize in Literature for his "wide cultural perspective and ... poetic overtones fashioning the drama of existence." His book, *The Man Died: Prison Notes*, is a 1972 non-fiction book that explores Soyinka's experiences in prison during the Nigerian Civil War. In 1984, a Nigerian court banned the book.

Soyinka has been imprisoned several times for his criticism of the government, and since the 1970s, he has lived long periods in exile.

More recently, there was a group of five activists of the Just Stop Oil environmental campaign who were handed years of prison sentences for their involvement in organizing peaceful protests that blocked a major London highway in 2022.

Greenpeace UK's program director Amy Cameron called the outcome a "dark day for the right to protest, a pillar of our democracy."

And in Cambodia, in early 2024, 10 activists from a local environmental group called Mother Nature were on trial at the Phnom Penh Capital Court. The charges stemmed from Mother Nature's public and peaceful protests that began in 2012. Through raising awareness and working with frontline human rights activists, they hope to protect Cambodia's environment.

In short, our systems are failing us.

So what do we do when the systems try to silence us?
We use them.

LESSON #93: USE THE SYSTEM TO WORK FOR US

There is a positive lesson out of all of this. Change is possible. In recent years, several landmark court cases around the world have set important precedents in holding governments and corporations accountable for their contributions to climate change. These cases have often been driven by environmental groups, activists, and concerned citizens, leading to significant legal victories for climate action. I'll share three examples, and take note on how different each angle is: one case is aimed at the corporate sector, one is led by women targeting their human rights and health risks, and the other is youth-led.

Milieudefensie et al. v. Royal Dutch Shell 2021)

Jurisdiction: Netherlands
Outcome: The Hague District Court ordered Royal Dutch Shell to reduce its global carbon emissions by 45% by 2030, compared to 2019 levels.
Significance: This was a groundbreaking case as it held a private corporation directly accountable for its contribution to climate change. It set a powerful precedent for future climate litigation against multinational corporations.

KlimaSeniorinnen Schweiz v. Swiss Federal Government (2016-2024)

Jurisdiction: Switzerland
Outcome: The European Court of Human Rights (ECHR) found that Switzerland failed to implement sufficient climate policies – violating the women's human rights.
Significance: This case, brought by the association KlimaSeniorinnen Schweiz (Senior Women for Climate Protection Switzerland), represents a landmark in climate litigation for its focus on the specific vulnerabilities of elderly women to climate change.

Juliana v. United States (2015-ongoing)

Jurisdiction: United States
Outcome: While not yet conclusively resolved, the case has seen several important decisions that recognize the potential for constitutional claims related to climate change.
Significance: Filed by 21 young plaintiffs, the case argues that the federal government's actions contributing to climate change violate their constitutional rights to life, liberty, and property. Although the case has faced procedural hurdles, it has brought significant attention to the rights-based approach to climate litigation.

All three examples above are of court cases that are making a huge dent in the political systems when it comes to topics like climate change! And that's just three examples; there are so many more.

In 2019, a group of 27 students from the University of the South Pacific came together to begin a campaign to persuade the leaders of the Pacific Islands Forum to take the issue of climate change and human rights to the International Court of Justice. Think about it for a second: a bunch of island kids coming together to take the climate crisis to the world's highest court. It's pretty cool, you can learn more about their work through The Worlds Youth for Climate Justice.

My greatest hope is for Indonesia to one day recognize and allow our dual nationality. We want to work hand in hand to better the future of our country. Creating an easier path for us to choose our Indonesian nationality will help us continue to do the good work many of us started.

There is so much power behind these personal human stories that allows us to gain insights into these large movements. But that's also one of the greatest faults of our systems: putting one person on the pedestal to receive all the praise and all the blame.

Systems are the foundations we stand on to do this work. They can either amplify or anchor our solutions. The current institutions are failing us. I believe this movement of change is outgrowing the systems in place. People power is more powerful than people in power. Read that again.

To quote Greenpeace UK's program director Amy Cameron again as she reflected more on the five Just Stop Oils activists sentenced to years in prison for peaceful protest, she said: "We're giving a free hand to the polluting elite robbing us of a habitable planet while jailing those who're trying to stop them – it makes no sense."

So, to make it make sense, we have to imagine new and better and fairer and more circular systems. The system we have now is outdated, unjust, and contributing to the acceleration of a dying planet.

We need to imagine a new system.

CHAPTER TEN:

AN INVITATION FOR THE WORLD

Lessons in this chapter:

#94: Hope is an action word

#95: The one-meter bubble

#96: Change starts with you

#97: You start to change too

#98: Endings can be beginnings too

#99: There isn't one way to be a changemaker

#100: Change starts now

A poem written in 2024
I was 23 years old

What if it all works out?
Even better than we had all hoped and planned
So much better than we could've even dreamed
What if the forests grow back
And the rivers flow full
And the bees
And the extinct rhinos, lizards, and polar bears
All came back
And Earth was home once again to all living species
What if it all works out? Even better than we had all hoped and planned
So much better than we could've even dreamed

"Close your eyes and visualize the world you want. What does that world look like?"

I was in a workshop and the lead facilitator was guiding us through an exercise where we had to imagine the world we want. "You can come up with anything, the wildest dreams come true here!" Afterwards, we opened our eyes and had to write it all down. The more detailed the better.

My world has lots of big trees, fresh, clean rivers, butterflies, and bees. I saw beautiful sunshine powering our buildings with light, gardens everywhere providing everyone with fresh food. Community-led action was at the center of every decision, and young people, of course, were actively involved.

The point of this exercise was that if we can't imagine a better system, a better world, how are we supposed to create one? It's hard to work towards something you can't see, feel, or touch.

Dreaming big is key. But making it tangible allows us to see results. And when we see results, we build the confidence and courage we need to keep on expanding our imagination for a better world.

Gloria Steinem once said, "Without leaps of imagination or dreaming, we lose the excitement of possibilities. Dreaming, after all, is a form of planning."

When my sister and I set out to make Bali plastic bag free, people said it was an impossible goal. But slowly, we started. We built a team and momentum. After each cleanup, we felt a success. After each government meeting, we felt a little closer to the goal. Every single signature we collected, donation we secured, event we spoke at: all of these tangible small goals made us realize that change was at our fingertips!

When I started YOUTHTOPIA, people said the vision was too big. They didn't "see" it. But I could feel it. And so did other young changemakers who helped build YOUTHTOPIA into what it is today. I knew it was the natural next step to create a platform for more young people to learn from each other. So, slowly we started. Just like Bye Bye Plastic Bags, we started to build momentum. Programs were developed. The learning platform was built. The community was created. Finally, people could start to see it too.

Both missions grew and, like the saying goes, all good things take time. But we all know that we do not have the luxury of time. We're running out of time. And most days, I feel like the world is also running out of hope. Next to the burnouts and the climate anxiety, there is so much heaviness and a sense of no hope.

In a TED Talk by journalist Angus Hervey, he explains to us that hope is an active exercise. "Hope isn't a noun. It is a verb. It is not something that we have or something that we are given. It is something that we do."

LESSON #94: HOPE IS AN ACTION WORD

That perspective changes everything. Hope is an activity: something we need to actively create space and time for. Just like brushing your teeth in the morning or getting dressed for work, hope has to become an exercised new norm.

"Doing hope" with other people can make it easier.

Climate joy

"If I can't dance, I don't want to join your revolution." I heard this for the first time when I listened to changemaker Dominique Palmer talk onstage. It was cold, and we were outside for a climate storytelling lab. Here, she was talking about the exact opposite of Climate Anxiety: Climate Joy. It was so simple and so inspiring. It was the beginning for so many people to join the climate movement.

Climate activist Leah Thompson said that joy can be seen as a practice of activism. It is a sign of active resistance to fall into the narrative that we are doomed. I believe it is a choice every day that we can make. There is power in that. So, dance and choose to be joyful.

After all, without things like joy and inspiration, where would we be? Nowhere. We would literally be nowhere. Joy leads to community. Inspiration sparks curiosity. Curiosity leads to innovation. Innovation is how we end up with lights that turn on and off and how I can type these words right now for you to read and hold in front of you. Hello! And to think it all starts with someone at some point being inspired.

I always find it easier to break things down, make it more tangible so I can understand the inspiration and go through to implementation. So let me introduce you to the One-Meter Bubble Concept.

Starting at 12 years old allows you to see things in a simple way. We don't have the ability to make things complicated yet. It is what it is. And speaking to many young people and adults, I recognized the anxiety of the task ahead: how were we going to get out of this mess?

Immediately, the fear of sacrificing something or having to change the way we do things would kick in. It all feels overwhelming. *This is too much for me. I can't do this. I am not a changemaker.* All those thoughts come up and keep us from becoming a part of the movement. When, in fact, (by now you know) that we need everybody. We need YOU.

LESSON #95: THE ONE-METER BUBBLE

This lesson is all about breaking things down. We know things are overwhelming and sometimes seem hard to focus on or achieve. So we break things down.

The one-meter bubble concept is an idea that you walk around with this imaginary bubble of one meter around you.

1 meter to the left, 1 meter to the right, 1 meter above and below.

Everything that comes within contact of your one-meter bubble is your responsibility to take care of.

Make sure it's not polluted and clean, make sure that everyone and everything feels safe and respected. And this bubble follows you everywhere you go. In every room you are in: your kitchen,

ONE METER BUBBLE

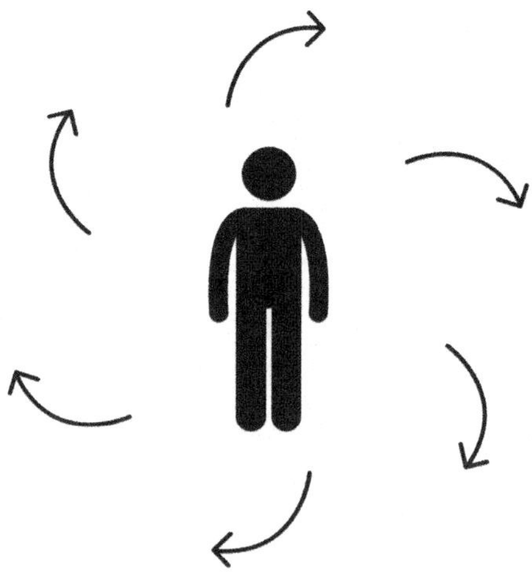

your classroom, your boardroom. It follows you in every vehicle: the public bus, a taxi, an Uber, train, or plane.

Imagine the world we would live in if everyone took care of just that one-meter bubble around them. Suddenly, it doesn't seem so daunting after all, does it?

LESSON #96: CHANGE STARTS WITH YOU

LESSON #97: YOU START TO CHANGE TOO

The sun was slowly dipping under the horizon. The day was coming to an end. I sat at the beach where I always tried to either start or end my days. The wind was hot, and the palm trees were glowing in the last light of the sun. *This is really my favorite place on Earth.*

I think about the road I had to walk on to get to the beach. So much has changed in these last few years. It used to be a path that farmers cut out for us through the rice field. We would wear shoes and long pants so our legs wouldn't be cut by the sharp stalks. With our swimming suits in the bags on our backs, my sister and I would run the whole way, screaming and squirming as we hoped we wouldn't step on a snake or scorpion.

Then, the road changed, and the way to the beach became a small dirt path, wide enough for the occasional motorbike to pass through the rice field. We wore shorts and dresses and were barefoot as we ran to the beach. The farmers stayed busy on their land growing rice. We knew each season of harvest the rice was at because we could see it.

Then, it changed again, and the path became a bit bigger for two motorbikes to cross each other. Land to the left and right of the path started to sell. Farmers were becoming few. We were on our motorbikes at this point, with our swimmers already on.

Then, it changed again, and now cars and trucks could pass on this road to the beach. All the land to the left and right of our little dirt path was sold, and there was not a single piece left for rice to grow. Nobody knew what season of harvest it was anymore.

So much has changed. I sat on the beach and looked behind me at the parking lot full of motorcycles. *This is ridiculous.* I look at the beach I grew up on. This beach that used to be quiet and empty with fallen stars on it was now covered with bean bags, cigarette ash, way too many rescue dogs, and a bunch of people who didn't know what season of harvest it was.

So much has changed. I took a sip of my coconut water and started to wonder: *How much have I changed? And how good or bad is the change?*

More than half of my life has been dedicated to this movement. I'm so incredibly proud and grateful and honored. All the feelings sometimes feel too big to carry.

But I also am beginning to realize that I know almost nothing else.

I am a founder. I am a speaker. I am an author. I am a student. I am young, I am old. I am 12, and I am 22, all at the same time.

I have lost my way multiple times along this journey. Sometimes it's good, sometimes it's scary, but it's always necessary. I call it:

The evolution of a changemaker

I've learned so much already and continue learning every single day.

The latest lesson I had to learn was knowing when to step back. As I've said before: starting is easy, continuing is hard. But ending it? Now that's a totally different level. In going through this next phase, I learned:

LESSON #98: ENDINGS CAN BE BEGINNINGS TOO

This was the hardest decision of my professional career and personal journey – deciding to close a chapter of my life; shutting down the daily operations of the project I had started with so much passion and energy.

We very rarely talk about endings on a positive note. It is usually attached with some fear, anxiety, and definitely the guaranteed nostalgic feeling that comes with endings. But sometimes, endings should be celebrated. In the case of Bye Bye Plastic Bags, that was exactly what we wanted to do.

After a decade of frontline actions, we realized that an entire movement of eco-warriors had grown on the island and throughout Indonesia. There were organizations active on a daily basis, cleaning the rivers, focusing on education, rallying with the government. Our movement, put bluntly, was not really doing much anymore. Of course, the history will always be a foundation of inspiration, but on a daily operations basis, it wasn't achieving the impact of the other organizations. Which is a good thing.

This was a celebration in my eyes because it meant that what we started began a life of its own. People heard the rallying cry and joined the movement in their own way. A beautiful ecosystem of partners and new organizations continue the work on plastic pollution in Bali.

The strength of Bye Bye Plastic Bags being youth-led still continues through our global teams and their youth leaders, from Taiwan to Surabaya, South Korea, and Singapore. But the day-to-day actions on Bali have come to an end. It was a big decision, and one I sat with for months, almost a full year. When I finally announced my decision, it felt like a weight lifted off my shoulders.

Where one door closes, another opens.

I have changed since I started Bye Bye Plastic Bags. And this is the celebration of endings for me. On a personal note, it created space for new things to grow!

Today, I'm a full-time changemaker. My goal in life is to ignite every single young person to feel like they have access to the same opportunities, tools, and community I had when I was 12 years old. I want to help invite as many people, young and old, towards this movement for a more sustainable, peaceful, and fair world. The hope I feel is contagious and I want to share as much of it as possible. The most exciting thing about all of this, you can find in the next lesson.

LESSON #99: THERE ISN'T ONE WAY TO BE A CHANGEMAKER

Being a changemaker looks different for everyone. There isn't one way to be a changemaker. There is no right or wrong way to get started in creating positive change. You don't have to start your own movement or take to the streets. You don't have to be a great public speaker or a founder of your own organization.

Use the tools you have around you. Implement the skills and the unique strengths you can bring to the movement. What stories and truths do you have access to that others don't? Who is in your network? What things are happening locally around you? What is missing, and how can you be a part of it?

We need artists, journalists, researchers, and scientists. We need people who love to study numbers, and those that are really good at social media. We need lawyers and healthcare professionals. All of our unique skills and strengths are needed in this movement to change our world. We need you. We need all of us. If previously, you did not feel invited to join, consider this your invitation from a full-time changemaker.

Change Starts With You.

Change Starts Now.

LESSON #100: CHANGE STARTS NOW.

ACKNOWLEDGEMENTS & GRATITUDE

This book is so much more than pages with words or lessons learned. Writing this book for the last year has been an adventure through 21 cities, a broken heart, a move to the other side of the world, a 35 kilometer race, and what feels like a thousand rounds of edits. Honestly, this book is a living, breathing project of its own. It is a collection of memories past, present, and a hope for the future.

Actually, now that I'm writing this, I find that it's true what they say: it is a bit daunting to write your first acknowledgement, because there are so many people to thank. It isn't just about the people who helped with this book: it is also about the people who supported you to become who you are today, from the very beginning. The people, places, and moments that shaped a 12-year-old girl to be a full-time changemaker today.

And perhaps, before the list of people begins, there are two places that deserve deep gratitude.

First, Bali. I will forever be an island girl. Terima Kasih Bali for the magic and wonder you have given me, and for all the lessons you continue to share. The family you have given me with Yuni, Made, Kadek, and Emy. And a word of thanks for the support of all local leaders and partners on the island.

And secondly, thank you to Amsterdam, too, for becoming my

second home. In the cold and gray, between the canals and the good weathered days, I welcome all the things I never knew were possible. Let the city surprise me.

To start at the start

Thank you to the Barges, the Stewarts, the Crezee, Ganzert and Hearn families, and the very first team members of Bye Bye Plastic Bags, Noel, Noor, Aqil, Dara, Lily Daskalov, Sara Soulier. You know who you are. I wouldn't be the person I am today without you.

Thank you to my teachers, Pak Glenn, Ibu Vicky, Pak Sal, Ibu Emily, Ibu Nicola, Pak Dan Ibu Desak, Ibu Kadek and so many more for always challenging me to go further, and then sometimes pulling me back down to Earth to do missed homework when the world of changemaking got too intense.

To the very first believers, John and Cynthia Hardy, who saw the vision from day one and supported the crazy ideas! I was inspired and supported by the world's best visionaries.

Karina, Tika, Esta, Rhea, Daan, Freya, Momoko, the interns team, and so many more for being some of the best people I had the pleasure to work with. You taught me so much about team work, building a vision together and getting things done.

Gary, for being there at the start and for everything we've been through together.

Flore, Dorothee, and the Bigger Than Us family: thank you for taking me into the world of film and bursting my plastic bubble. And for friendship for life: Mo, Mary, Winnie, Memory, Rene, Xiuhtezcatl.

To the present moment

To my forever HQ team, thank you Lily for stepping up and upholding our to-do list when I needed to write, cry, or just be. I am so grateful for you. Working with you is my favorite part. Tomo, for being the best art director of all time and for reminding everyone to stay funky. Charles, for being the best videographer and editor and dancer and HQ bodyguard.

Thank you Nicholas for reminding me a page a day is successful enough and for my favorite couch in the city, where I submitted the very first draft from.

Thank you to my girls all around the world, MMIS in Bangkok and Milan, Hot Grandmas in Bali, and the BBB Babies in Holland, for the sleepovers and mini reading out loud sessions, the parties and hugs, and everything in between.

Thank you Stuart Sullivan for always translating my vision into design, from the YOUTHTOPIA logo to the cover of this book. Thank you especially for this cover, which was designed on a boat out at sea with barely any connection after our one or two calls, and yet, the final design was perfect.

Thank you Carmen Kemmink, for capturing my energy in a photo on my favourite place on earth, my childhood beach.

Thank you to my mentors:

Chris, for teaching me so much about focus, and how the world can work if you just think big enough: "Dream bigger, kid."

Bruno, thank you for always inspiring me with the power of a good conversation. Recently you reminded me to allow space for new and better; and it's up to us.

Maria, for the superpower of connecting people and guiding me through the world of explorers, from city to city.

Thank you to all the local and international stages that gave this story a platform. Thank you to the partners who believed in us and made it all happen. Special thanks to Hans Janssen, who made it possible for me to open for President Barack Obama, which was the beginning of this book turning into a reality, with the team of HarperCollins in the audience of 9,000 people.

Thank you Els for the trust in this book and for the trust in me as a writer, and the patience you showed me when my vision took time to translate into words. Julia, Lisanne, Alice, Erwin, and the whole HarperCollins team. Thank you for the guidance in edits and revisions and for the countless hours working together to make this book come to life.

And finally, a wholehearted thank you to my family, to which I owe everything to.

My sister, Bel: you drive me crazy, but I love you with everything I've got. And thank you for all the meals you cooked to show you care and for the hugs (those special hugs!) and sister sleepovers!

Thank you to my parents, who always saw my potential before I even saw it myself.

My papa for reminding me to go with the flow and that everything will be okay. Thank you for always being there, no matter what. And for being so proud of me, no matter what.

My mama for encouraging me to focus on everything that is possible, for all the warm cups of tea and plates of food so that I could sit, not move, and just write. I know I don't say it enough but, thank you for everything.

My heart is filled with deep gratitude. I feel as though this book is the closing of a chapter, an end of an era, as well as the start of something new.

How bittersweet. How nostalgically exciting.

Thank you everyone – past, present, and those I have yet to meet!

EXTRA

WRITTEN REFLECTIONS

Exercising our imagination is a lifelong choice. Each day, and in each moment, we can decide to grow our imagination. How do changemakers do it? Well, in conversation with some of the most creative thinkers, I see a common thread throughout their personalities. They are extremely creative humans, but they are people of deep reflection, too. The combination of art and mindfulness are core pillars in their DNA structure. They know who they are.

"How does this make you feel?"

"Does it feel like a step in the right direction?"

"What is the definition of success to you?"

This segment invites you to reflect on a series of questions catered to help guide you through a deep, inward dive of what world you envision for the future and right now. And don't worry if you're not a writer: that's okay. Maybe try answering these questions in conversation with someone you're close to. The purpose of this reflection journey is to reflect inwards because you first have to become aware of YOU before YOU can dream of a better world.

If you would like help getting in the zone, I can suggest the incredible tool of YOUTHTOPIA, where we created a guided meditation. But not just any guided meditation. This one was created by changemakers for changemakers, with the purposeful intent to slow down amidst a busy schedule.

Take a listen to the guided meditation.

Remember there is no specific order that you need to answer the questions, and for this exercise, there is no right or wrong answer. Just write as you feel.

What do you think the world needs right now?

What are your core values? How do they influence your decisions and actions?

If you were a teacher, what would you teach in your class?

What is one moment where you felt the most amount of hope?

How did you overcome your biggest challenge?

Tell us about someone who you look up to?

What is a piece of advice that has stuck with you?

What do you believe is the most harmful myth towards the youth movement?

If you could turn back time, where would you go, and what would you do?

On a bad day, how do you find your motivation again?

What do you love the most about your community?

What do you love most about our world?

RESOURCE LIBRARY

5 TED Talks you should watch

Let Curiosity Lead by Yara Shahid

How Great Leaders Inspire Action by Simon Sinek

Do Schools Kill Creativity? by Sir Ken Robinson

The Disarming Case to Act Now on Climate Change by Greta Thunberg

Why You Should Be a Climate Activist by Luisa Neubauer

5 documentaries to be inspired by

Bigger Than Us by Flore Vassuer

Rising Up by Kal Glaznig

The Way of the Whale by Xiye Beara and Francisco Campos-Lopez Benyunes

Yumi by World's Youth for Climate Justice

Kiss the Ground by Joshua Tickell & Rebecca Harrell Tickell

4 podcasts to learn from

Diary of a CEO by Steven Bartlett

Happenus by Shawn Hung

Women Emerging by Julia Middleton

A Slight Change of Plans by Maya Shankar

4 grants to apply to

Iris Prize

Re Earth Initiative

YOUTHTOPIA Mini Grants

Youth Climate Justice Fund

10 organizations to get to know

AimHi Earth

Waterbear Networks

The Cacao Project

Force of Nature

Arkipelago Mundo

Climate Cardinals

Yayasan Haka

Youth Demand

Astungkara Way

Hero

10 top YOUTHTOPIA programs

Public Speaking with Melati and Isabel Wijsen

Climate Anxiety Masterclass with Clover Hogan

Indigenous Storytelling Masterclass with Janali Dancaster

How to Build Better Habits with Melati Wijsen

How to Run for Politics with Sophie Handford

How to Debate with Angelyna Victoria

Extreme Weather with the Hogeschool in Utrecht

How to Build Communities with Mohamad Aljounde

How to Navigate Taboos with Faye Simanjuntak

Kembali ke Hutan Documentary

100 CHANGEMAKERS TO LEARN FROM

Remember that changemaking is a lifelong journey, and those who can help us along the way to improve and reach our individual and collective potential are other changemakers. Here is a list of humans I look up to, and I hope will inspire you to keep on learning too.

1. Aakash Ranison
2. Abigail Limuria
3. Aishwarya Sridhar
4. Alison Bellewood
5. Andhyta F. Utami (Afu)
6. Andrew Kalaweit
7. Ann Makosinski
8. Aqil Reza
9. Autumn Peltier
10. Ayisha Siddiqa
11. Bibi-Jane Angelica
12. Bisan Owda
13. Bruno Giussani
14. Camille Etienne
15. Chitra Subyakto
16. Christiana Figueres
17. Clover Hogan
18. David Attenbourough
19. Deepak Chopra
20. Denica Riadini-Flesch
21. Disha Ravi
22. Dominique Palmer
23. Ed Jackson
24. Ellen Windemuth
25. Farwiza Farhan
26. Fionn Ferreira
27. Flore Vasseur
28. Gab Mejia
29. Gary Bencheghib
30. Grace Forrest
31. Greta Thunberg
32. Gro Brundtland

33. Helena Gualinga
34. Iman Usman
35. Ines Prada
36. Isaias Hernadez
37. Isabel Wijsen
38. Issa Barte
39. Jack Johnson
40. JC Felic
41. Jamie Margolin
42. Jane Goodall
43. Jojo Mehta
44. Kevin Handojo
45. Kevin Patel
46. Kinvara Jardine Paterson
47. Koteka Wenda
48. Laetania Belai Djandam
49. Lara Rudar
50. Laya Pothunuri
51. Lily Lim
52. Louise Mabulo
53. Luisa Neubauer
54. Maia Penn
55. Malala Yousafzai
56. Malin Fezehai
57. Maria Chan
58. Mary Finn
59. Maya Penn
60. Memory Banda
61. Merijn Everaarts
62. Mert Kumru
63. Mia Motley
64. Mikaela Loach
65. Mitzi Jonelle Tan
66. Mohamad Al Jounde
67. Nadya Okamoto
68. Nala Amirah
69. Nathan Metenier
70. Notep
71. Nyombi Morris
72. Olivina Maskan
73. Pamela Ea
74. Paloma Costa
75. Princess Laurentien of the Netherlands
76. Qiyun Woo
77. Rene Silva
78. Ritika Saraswat
79. Sage Lenier
80. Sandrayati Faye
81. Sophia Handford
82. Sophia Kianni
83. Sophia Skarparis
84. Sônia Guajajara
85. Stephanie Dickson
86. Sophie Handford
87. Suluafi Brianna Fruean

88. Tasha Tanjutco
89. Tiana Day
90. Tiza Mafira
91. Toby Thorpe
92. Tori Tsui
93. Vandana Shiva
94. Vanessa Nakate
95. Varsha Yajman
96. Wawa Gatheru
97. Winnie Tushabe
98. Xiuhtezcatl Martinez
99. Xiye Bastida
100. Yvon Chouinard

THE 100 LESSONS FROM CHANGE STARTS NOW

In summary, here are the 100 lessons from this book. Remember, this is just the starting point. If I'm being honest, I could have written a hundred more! Life is always a continuous learning journey after all.

CHAPTER ONE LESSONS

#1: We are nature
#2: We protect what we love
#3: Balance between good and bad creates harmony
#4: Trí Hita Karana
#5: Feeling safe allows you to explore
#6: Always ask questions
#7: Role Models Matter
#8: Find your focus
#9: Change takes time

CHAPTER TWO LESSONS

#10: It's worse than we think
#11: Time is ticking
#12: Trust change will happen
#13: Overcome climate Anxiety

#14: Think Big

#15: Don't be fooled by excuses

#16: Share your Knowledge

#17: Speak the language of Data

#18: Adjustments are good

#19: How to navigate community feedback

#20: Inaction is Expensive

#21: Change is the only constant

CHAPTER THREE LESSONS

#22: Petitions build momentum

#23: Creativity builds momentum

#24: Always have a clear call to action

#25: Fun builds momentum!

#26: Recognize your strengths

#27: Teams build momentum

#28: Titles make a difference

#29: Create a successful workflow

CHAPTER FOUR LESSONS

#30: Pivot when things aren't working

#31: An Office changes everything

#32: Dreams do come true

#33: Take your time, trust your gut

#34: Good ideas travel far

#35-44: 10 lessons on going global

#45: Do the things you want to do
#46: Choose your priorities, Manage distractions, & Make Decisions
#47: No big teams, just the right people
#48: You cannot do it alone

CHAPTER FIVE LESSONS

#49: Exercise your imagination
#50: Never underestimate the power of a good story
#51: Two ears, one mouth for a reason
#52: Public Speaking is a skill you can learn
#53: A good story has many ingredients
#54: Know Your Audience
#55: Change your narrative, not your goal
#56: Focus on your WHY
#57: If the story is there, everything else will follow
#58: Translating stories into income
#59: Sharing opportunities with others sparks joy
#60: Inspiration is where change begins

CHAPTER SIX LESSONS

#61: This is not a sacrifice
#62: Activism is not defined by age
#63: Changemaking is a lifestyle
#64: Be Present. Be your age. It's Okay.
#65: Experiences Shape Our Own Truths
#66: The world is changing

CHAPTER SEVEN LESSONS

#67: Greenwashing is so over

#68: Youthwashing happens, and it sucks

#69: Give, Go, Offer (the go with 2 g's)

#70: Our Differences can be our Strengths

#71: The power of mentors

#72-77: The do's & don't for finding a mentor

#78: How to establish a good collaboration

CHAPTER EIGHT LESSONS

#79: Don't let your Ego Take lead

#80: Honesty is the best policy

#81: Accept where you are right now

#82: Beware of burnout

#83: "It is a privilege to burn out"

#84: Stop being busy just to be busy

#85: You don't always have to have an answer

#86: Take care of your energy

CHAPTER NINE LESSONS

#87: Set yourself up for success

#88: Keep a diverse group around you

#89: Dating (as) a changemaker

#90: Practice self-love

#91: You are not your passport

#92: Systems are designed to fail us

#93: Use the system to work for us

CHAPTER TEN LESSONS

#94: Hope is an action word

#95: The one-meter bubble

#96: Change starts with you

#97: You start to change too

#98: Endings can be beginnings too

#99: There isn't one way to be a changemaker

#100: Change starts now

BIBLIOGRAPHY

Chapter Two

Carbon Disclosure Project. Carbon Majors Report: 100 Companies Responsible for 71% of Global Greenhouse Gas Emissions, 2017.

IPCC. Sixth Assessment Report (AR6). https://www.ipcc.ch/assessment-report/ar6/.

World Resources Institute. "Assessing Progress on NDCs." https://www.wri.org/insights/assessing-progress-ndcs.

United Nations Statistics Division. Progress Chart: 17 Sustainable Development Goals, 2023. https://unstats.un.org/sdgs/report/2023/progress-chart/Progress-Chart-2023.pdf.

International Labour Organization. Working on a Warmer Planet: The Effect of Heat Stress on Productivity and Decent Work. https://www.ilo.org/publications/major-publications/working-warmer-planet-effect-heat-stress-productivity-and-decent-work.

AON. Weather, Climate, and Catastrophe Insight: 2023 Report. https://www.aon.com/getmedia/f34ec133-3175-406c-9e0b-25ce-a768c5cf/20230125-weather-climate-catastrophe-insight.pdf.

Climate Policy Initiative. "The Cost of Inaction: USD 5.4 Trillion to USD 11.7 Trillion PerYear Until 2030." https://www.climatepolicyinitiative.org/the-cost-of-inaction/#:~:text=CPI%20estimates%20that%20climate%20finance.

Chapter Five

Sinek, Simon. "The Golden Circle." https://simonsinek.com/golden-circle/.

MasterClass. "How to Use the 7-38-55 Rule to Negotiate Effectively." https://www.masterclass.com/articles/how-to-use-the-7-38-55-rule-to-negotiate-effectively.

Chapter Six

Carrington, Damian. "Whole Foods CEO John Mackey: Climate Change Is Not Bad." The Guardian, January 18, 2013. https://www.theguardian.com/environment/2013/jan/18/whole-foods-ceo-climate-change-bad.

University of Cambridge. The Dasgupta Review: Economics of Biodiversity. https://www.cam.ac.uk/stories/dasguptareview.

HuffPost. "85% of Jobs That Will Exist in 2030 Haven't Been Invented Yet." HuffPost Canada. https://www.huffpost.com/archive/ca/entry/85-of-jobs-that-will-exist-in-2030-haven-t-been-invented-yet-d_ca_5cd4e7dae4b07bc72973112c.

Chapter Seven

Jackman, Josh. "Worst Examples of Greenwashing." The Eco Experts. https://www.theecoexperts.co.uk/news/worst-examples-of-greenwashing?cid=5b23dc1156f7a.

Prudente, Gianna. "98% of Gen Z Workers Are Dealing with Burnout Symptoms. Here's Why." LinkedIn. https://www.linkedin.com/pulse/98-gen-z-workers-dealing-burnout-symptoms-heres-cause-gianna-prudente-xocgf/.

We Are Family Foundation. "Collaborating Across Generations: Intergenerational Report." https://study.wearefamilyfoundation.org/.

Printed in Dunstable, United Kingdom

67924583R00180